FIFTY LIVES FOR GOD

FIFTY LIVES
FOR GOD

15660

Cyril Davey

JUDSON PRESS

Valley Forge

© *Cyril Davey 1973*

Published in 1973 by OLIPHANTS, Marshall, Morgan & Scott
Judson Press edition published in 1974

Library of Congress Cataloging in Publication Data

Davey, Cyril James.
    Fifty lives for God.

    1. Christian biography. I. Title.
BR1700.2.D35   209'.22 [B]   73-13450
ISBN 0-8170-0629-X

Printed in the U.S.A.

ACKNOWLEDGEMENTS

Most of the material for the sketches in this book has been accumulated, some of it over a long period, in notebooks, paper-cuttings and in my own memory. It is impossible to make either full or faithful acknowledgement for a great deal of what is written. The sketches themselves are, indeed, so brief that in many cases fifteen hundred words may derive from half a dozen different sources. In very few instances have I turned only to a single standard biography and sifted out the facts convenient to the story.

I would wish, however, to acknowledge my indebtedness in the following cases. So far as the rest are concerned they fall into the broad categories mentioned in the first paragraph.

I am grateful to the World Council of Churches for material about Samuel Amissah and Annie Ruth Jiagge; to the Rev. G. Eric Firth for information about U Ba Ohn; to Marshall, Morgan and Scott for permission to use their books on John Beekman, Bob Harrington, Dale Evans Rogers and Oswald J. Smith; to the Rev. Dr Cyril H. Powell and Arthur James Ltd., for permission to use material about Lilian Baylis; to the British Ludhiana Fellowship for information about Edith Brown; to the Cheshire Foundation for Homes for the Sick for some of the facts about Leonard Cheshire's later work; to published material of the British Pestalozzi Children's Village Association for some facts about the village; to the Rev Ormonde McConnell for the sight of a manuscript about Marco Dépestre; to the Baptist Missionary Society for an article about Ina Disengomoka; to Hodder and Stoughton for permission to use facts from *Archibald the Arctic*, and to the author's executors; to the Australian High Commission for supplying copy material about John Flynn and about the Royal Flying Doctor Service; to the British and Foreign Bible Society for information about Evangeline French; to the Epworth Press and the author, Roy Belmer, for permission to use material from his biography of Annie James, *The Teeth of the Dragon;* to the Save the Children Fund for information about that Fund and its founder, Eglantine Jebb; to the Salvation Army for the use of its own published material about Kawl Khuma and Charles Péan; to the Church's Ministry among the Jews for providing Eric Lipson's own story; to Wm. Collins, Sons & Co. for permission to use material from Chief Albert Luthuli's autobiography,

5

Let My People Go; to Hodder and Stoughton and the author, the
Rt. Rev. David Sheppard for permission to use material from
Parson's Pitch; to the Student Christian Movement and Werner Huhne,
author of *A Man To Be Reckoned With*, the biography of Reinold
von Thadden-Trieglaff; and to Wm Collins, Sons & Co. and Malcolm Muggeridge, author of *Something Beautiful for God*, the story
of Mother Teresa.

No quotations infringing copyright have been used, so far as I am
aware, but if facts or incidents have been included for which permission should have been sought, I offer my apologies.

CYRIL DAVEY

CONTENTS

Contents

8

Contents

9

Contents

CHRIS

We knew of Christopher for some four years before we actually met him. John, his father, was a 'regular', a 'back-room boy' at Wesley Lodge, the manse where we spent three intensely happy years in New Delhi in the middle of the last war. No one was more concerned than John to offer friendship to newcomers, to take his share in the chores of putting out supper and washing up on Sunday evenings when the manse seemed likely to burst its sides with service-men and -women. Like most of those who were with us, John's thoughts fled homewards when we sang and prayed each Sunday evening: 'Holy Father . . . keep our loved ones . . ., 'neath Thy care.'

John had specially good reasons for thinking of them—his wife and his two small sons. Chris, the elder, had a heart complaint.

He might well live until his father got home—but, after that, how long? Until he was seven? Fourteen, perhaps?

If he lived, what could he do with his life? A 'blue baby', with a heart which any severe stress or physical energy might try beyond endurance, the future was more than a little bleak for those who loved him.

Chris was still there when John got back after the war. When we visited them we found him a cheerful, friendly small boy, cared for but not coddled, protected but not held down. There was a tacit acceptance amongst their friends that he should enjoy as much of his life as he could. He enjoyed his clockwork motor-cars, his train set, but when his smaller brother went out to play there was little that Chris could do except watch, if anything really energetic were on hand. Toy cars, yes—but no real ones for Chris in the days to come, Drawing engines—but no drawing-board in an office, Other small boys and girls to tea—but no home of his own for Chris. As much fun as he could manage—but presumably a good deal of frustration.

If he lived that long . . .

Chris went on living. Not just existing, but really living.

At eight years old he had an operation. The results seemed to be negligible, but he gained a friend in the doctor, who never forgot him. In some way, however, though the operation failed to achieve all the famous and skilled surgeon set out to do, it seemed to have a rather odd result. It was as though Chris, thin, small and handicapped, made up his eight-year-old mind to do what nobody else could do for him. Why should 'something wrong with his heart' keep him out of life?

He had to go to a special school for children with handicaps like his own. He quickly proved there was nothing wrong with his mind, and he showed a special interest in mechanical affairs.

Other small boys joined the Scouts. Why shouldn't he? Chris found a place in a troop of handicapped scouts.

So it went on.

He didn't conquer his heart-trouble, but he lived with it, and learned that he could do much more than anyone had believed possible.

No job when he left school? He found a job, and kept it, in a firm which dealt with ventilation and dust-extraction plant. That he was kept on, year after year, was no charitable act of generous employers. He showed his worth, and proved it highly.

No car of his own? This year he was driving a mini-Cooper—round England, down to the West Country, up through the Highlands.

No girl friend? He married a charming and courageous young school-teacher. His home life was full and natural, with two baby girls to enrich it.

But that was not the whole of his life, by any means. In a part-Anglican, part-Methodist home Chris went to a Baptist Sunday school because it was nearest. When the family moved he became involved with the parish church Sunday school. As he grew into a teenager and then into his twenties, he not only shared in all the youth activities but found that many of them were revolving round him. He helped run the youth club. He was interested in drama. He sang in the choir and in the choral society. Wherever he was, things happened. Whatever he did, was done well and successfully. In whatever group he was found there was an air of cheerfulness and gaiety.

'Happy . . . gay . . . cheerful . . . friendly . . . thoughtful for others . . . uncomplaining . . . optimistic . . .

'A real Christian.'

These were the things I heard people saying about him outside the church at Claygate, as well as in the brief tribute a friend paid to him at his funeral service. For, at last, other disabilities besides his heart trouble brought his gay and courageous life to an end. Just over three weeks ago, as I write this, I was privileged to share in the last prayers by which we committed his earthly body to the elements and his life to God who gave it.

But there is something wrong about that phrase. It was not we who, at the end, committed Chris to God. He himself had done that long ago. That is why, at the beginning of this book, I thought it good to pay tribute to him.

In speaking of Chris, whom many of us loved, I speak of a great multitude of other people.

This book has an apt title, suggested by Peter Lardi, its publisher. *Fifty Lives for God.*

Chris

Here are the stories of men and women who have touched life with glory. They range from priests and Salvation Army officers to soldiers and explorers. They come from nearly thirty different countries and gave Christian service in a dozen more. They represent almost all the main denominations, though some belonged to large or small evangelical groups which owned no ecclesiastical tradition. They have been engaged in many kinds of Christian witness and service. Though not all are now alive there are very few who have been dead for more than a decade.

They are triumphant proof that our theological divisions do not really represent, at any point, the wholeness of God, who declared Himself the Father of all men and the Saviour of all men for ever in Jesus Christ. In every continent, in every Church, in every area of life, God both empowers and honours His servants.

Fifty lives for God.

There could have been half a dozen books, each as varied, each as challenging.

But for every one of these fifty there are ten thousand, a million people indeed, whose lives were truly 'lives for God'.

Ordinary people, empowered and transformed by God.

People like Chris.

Cyril Davey

Epsom
1972

13

WITHOUT BITTERNESS

Any African who has grown up in the modern world has reason for thanksgiving. Africa has long ceased to be the 'dark continent'—and yet its leap forward is no more than a generation or so old. So much has been achieved in so short a time and, despite the highlighted failures, with so little violence that an African from Ghana, for instance, may well lift up his heart. He is part of a continent on the move.

At the same time, bitterness is hard to banish. In many parts of the continent, especially in Southern Africa, 'rights' are still described as 'privileges', given or withheld by a minority sometimes black, more often white. A man may be regarded as less than fully human because of the colour of his skin.

Samuel Hanson Amissah is an African of the modern world, a leader of the Church who has been exposed to scorn as well as praise. He is a man without bitterness.

A Methodist—for many Ghanaians belong to that Church—he was accepted for teacher-training at Wesley College and was asked to remain on the staff after he had graduated. In 1952 he became the first African principal of the college where he had trained. It was not a surprising choice. In the years between he had shown a deep understanding of what education should mean for the African people. It 'must underline those values which have stood the test of time and are deeply cherished by Africans—fellow-feeling, sharing what one has with others, a sensitivity to the other world . . . '

On his appointment as Supervisor of Methodist Schools in 1940 he was sent to London by his Church to study at the London University Institute of Education. It was a frightening journey, and an even more terrifying arrival. After a six weeks' voyage, dogged by submarines, he reached London when it was suffering the worst of the German air raids. The peril was vividly illustrated when a friend persuaded him one evening not to wait for a bus but to go back with him to his own lodgings. Next day he heard that a bomb had killed all those in the queue.

On his return to Africa, hurt by many things he saw and shared in Britain, but with his faith in God and his own mission unshaken, he quickly found himself involved in the affairs not only of his own Church but of all the Churches. Representing Methodism on the Christian Council of Ghana and in Church Union negotiations he was easily marked out as a man of deep faith, swift perception and broad vision. When the All-Africa Council of Churches met in Kampala, Uganda, in 1963, he was appointed its secretary.

A new appointment in a new Council in a rapidly changing Africa—what could he make of it? There were no precedents, and no one to guide him, God alone must direct him. He set out to create a programme for the Churches which would help them to share their insights, strengthen each other and begin to offer guidance and help to those who sought it. Working quietly behind the scenes, rather than setting out to become a public figure, he began to build a fellowship between Churches which hardly knew each other, and between the African Churches and the rest of the world.

He came to his office, and lived through it, in a period of turmoil. The Nigerian conflict strained the fellowship of the Church, but he refused to rush into mediation until both sides were prepared to accept it. In the southern Sudan, less publicised, the situation was bitter and intransigent. Here he sought to put pressure on the Sudanese government to accept its own responsibilities. In Rhodesia, with a fellow member of the A.A.C.C., he suffered the humiliations common to all black men, and was stopped and searched in a Salisbury street by policemen who offered neither reason nor excuse for doing so.

When he left his A.A.C.C. office in Nairobi in 1969, at the end of his term as secretary, he was a man known throughout the councils of the Church all over the world. Geneva knew him, and New York, and London, Asia and Eastern Europe. Indeed, instead of returning straight to Ghana, the plane from Nairobi took him to Moscow—to represent the Churches of Africa at the enthronement of the new Patriarch of the Russian Orthodox Church. It was his last official act in his old capacity.

Nothing he has seen or shared—the war which the white nations fought out across the world or the physical dangers he faced in the Nigerian conflict, the divisions of the Church or the struggle for power in his own land, the self-seeking men of many races or the narrowness of vision and concern amongst church people both black and white—has touched his soul with bitterness. Least of all has it destroyed his belief that God has great purposes for the Church in Africa.

THE LOTUS AND THE CROSS

'Through all the ages to come the Indian Church will rise up in gratitude to attest the heroism and self-denying labours of the missionary body. You have given your goods to feed the poor. You have given your bodies to be burned. We ask also for *love.* Give us *friends!*'

The year was 1910. The place, Edinburgh. The occasion, the first-ever World Missionary Conference. The speaker, Azariah, an Indian student-work secretary in his thirties, vigorous, clear-spoken and already much respected. To say such things in that year required immense courage, for the 'missions' dominated the Indian Christian scene. The western missionary very seldom regarded the Indian as in any sense his equal, and certainly did not open either his home or his heart to an Indian colleague. Azariah could only speak with any hope of his words being heard because he was not pleading for personal equality but was concerned primarily about the mission of the Church. Only in true colleagueship could the Gospel be effectively preached.

These things were profoundly true of Azariah. In some parts of his life he had had very close European colleagues, and he had been encouraged by them to believe that India itself, and the Indian people, had insights into the Gospel which a westerner could not have. In short, he saw that Indians must take much more responsibility for preaching and interpreting the word of Christ to their own people. His whole life was to prove how right he was.

He was born in 1874 in Tinnevelli (now known as Tirunelveli) and his parents were members of the Anglican church. His enduring love of the Bible he gained from his mother. His parents dedicated him without reserve to Christ, with a dream that one day he might be a pastor to his own people. From boarding school—Mission-run— he went to Madras Christian College, but he did not see his own future in terms of the ordained ministry. Instead, he became the Y.M.C.A. secretary for South India, thus beginning ten years of arduous student work. His brilliance as organiser and speaker made a swift rise in responsibility inevitable, and by 1907 he had visited Japan, for the World Student Christian Federation conference, and was that year elected vice-chairman of the Federation. His future seemed clear .

But already the currents which were to swing him in a very different direction had begun to affect the pattern of his life.

His colleague in Y.M.C.A. and student work was a notable

American Christian, Sherwood Eddy, and with him he developed a deep friendship which changed his attitude to the many patronising missionaries whom he met. It was Eddy, as much as anyone, who persuaded him that India had her own contribution to make to the life of the Church. It was with Eddy, too, that he went on a mission to Jaffna, in Ceylon, and discovered that the Jaffna church was sending Tamil missionaries to India. He was appalled to remember that his own church in Tinnevelli, rich in money and resources, was not engaged in mission work to any effective extent. By 1903 he was largely responsible for the creation of the Indian Missionary Society in Tinnevelli.

Bishop Whitehead of Madras, a man who shared Azariah's vision and found no problems in close friendship with him, chose Dornakal—a huge rural area described as having 'the most drunken and degraded devil-worshippers in India'—as the scene of the Society's work. Azariah offered to join the team himself. Most of his friends saw this as a deplorable waste of his gifts. Azariah heard it as the call of God, and turned away from the student world on which he had already made such impact. In 1909 he was ordained, and three years later appointed assistant Bishop of Madras.

To many people this was going much too far. India was not yet ready for Indian bishops. The white community was horrified. The Government opposed the idea. Some missionaries wrote that they would never serve under an Indian. One senior missionary sent him on his way with the hope that 'you will do as little harm as you can to the Church'!

Dornakal was to be Azariah's home for the remainder of his life.

On his appointment there were six clergy and 8,000 Christians in an area as large as Wales. Within five years both numbers had doubled. By 1920 the diocese had been extended to include an area as large as England and Wales together, with 90,000 Christians. Azariah was never free of problems—of discipline, of inadequate training, of too few clergy. His main anxiety was not that the Church did not grow, but that it grew so fast. This was the land of the 'mass movement', where not only whole families but whole villages entered the Church and it was a constant concern to provide adequate pastoral care and training. But Azariah's twin articles of faith served him well. They were: 'Always trust the Holy Spirit, and always trust men.'

The outcaste movement had its own positive results. The depraved Malas and Madigas were often so completely changed in character, and their villages transformed, that their caste masters began to follow them into the Church. Azariah, with his passionate zeal for evangelism, would make them put their hands on their own heads, reminding them of their baptism, and then make them repeat the Pauline injunction, 'Woe is me if I preach not the Gospel'. The new Christian, from the beginning, was expected to be a witness to his faith.

17

The Church grew—and it was an *Indian* Church, in which missionaries served but where they did not lead.

In politics Azariah was a convinced nationalist, though he denounced all forms of violence. His demand was simple. 'We ask the right to make our own mistakes.' His attitude to Church government was the same, but not on political grounds. Maturity came only with responsibility. His vision, however, was of the *Church*, not of a group of denominations. Throughout his life he laboured for unity, as well as for a Church which Indians would regard as their own.

The cathedral which he built in the still-remote town of Dornakal was completely Indian in style, architecture and decoration. The lotus, the symbol of Indian spirituality, and the cross, the sign of Christ, appear everywhere. Yet it was a Christian church, without compromise. Acceptance of Christ was a step into a new life, and the growing Christian community, not merely changed but transformed, was proof of Christ's renewing power.

The need for unity was underlined by Dr Ambedkar, who led a political movement of India's outcastes but refused to bring them into the Christian Church. 'This is to move from one set of divisions into another life of division.' To Azariah an Indian member of 'the Church of England', an Indian who called himself a 'Swedish Lutheran' or an 'American Baptist' was talking nonsense. He worked throughout his life for a united Church in South India.

It was born, the 'Church of South India', in 1947, a little less than three years after Azariah's death in his beloved Dornakal.

THE WOLF THAT NEVER SLEEPS

It was the Matabele people who gave to Baden-Powell the name *Impeesa*, 'the wolf that never sleeps'. It was their own tribute to an intelligence officer who fought against them in the rising of their people and who seemed to know as much about tracking, surprise and the ways of the wild as they did themselves. His later world-service derived, in the beginning, from those experiences.

Robert Baden-Powell, born in 1857, was in his middle eighties when he died and was buried amongst the uplands of Kenya, where his grave looks across the valley to the snows of Mount Kenya. Many men have lived more than one life; few have lived two lives so distinct yet inter-related, or begun a new career in their fifties which was to alter the history of men so dramatically.

School was hard discipline, with occasional lapses into slap-stick comedy when he used his considerable skill as an actor. Going into the Army instead of to Oxford after coming second in the cavalry examinations, his first twenty-five years of Service life were never short of interest or excitement. A spell in India, and then in South Africa, ended with a return to Britain.

Holidays on the continent led, for a while, to his becoming a spy, when his old passion for play-acting asserted itself. After a walking tour with his brother he went eastwards through Germany on his own. The Franco-German war was over—but what would follow next? Wearing an Austrian hat with a feather in the brim, with a walking stick, a limp and a curious German accent he turned into a Central European sightseer instead of a British Officer. He penetrated behind the German lines, watched the military manoeuvres and was a guest in an officers' mess before he was finally unmasked. Even then he managed to escape. He did so again when he penetrated a German dockyard and lay on top of a wall while his pursuers ran below it, as he had done on tree-branches to avoid detection in the woods at Charterhouse. As an artist in the Balkans, and in fishermen's clothing in the Dardanelles, he breached the defences of Eastern Europe and Turkey. It occurred to him from time to time that this was real *Boy's Own Paper* stuff—and how much the boys would have enjoyed it!

In the South African War spying was a more serious business, and more dangerous. He learned the secrets of the African trackers themselves, and often beat them at their own skills. He used his talents against the Boer armies. In a little manual intended for training intelligence officers in the Army he set down what he had learned, and published *Aids to Scouting*. Courage, intelligence, quick wits, an acquaintance with tracks, skies, maps and charts, a knowledge of animals and men were not merely aids but essentials, and they were all there.

It was in that war that Baden-Powell rose unknowingly to fame, for he was besieged in Mafeking with a civilian population and a tiny garrison for seven months. When he returned to England he was a hero. Everyone wanted to see him and listen to him. The boy's magazine, *Greyfriars*, persuaded him to write some articles and his name became even more widely known. He discovered that one of his talents was to interest boys and perhaps to inspire them to a new idealism. To his astonishment he found that the principal of a ladies' teacher-training college at Ambleside, in the Lake District, had got hold of a copy of his *Aids to Scouting* and was using it with her students.

So far these were merely different skeins of experience. It was the founder of another famous organisation who was to give the twist which would turn them into a rope with which B.P. would be bound to boys for ever.

Because he was not only a famous soldier but also an acknowledged Christian, he was invited to Glasgow to speak at a Boys' Brigade Rally. Afterwards he had long talks with William Smith, the founder of the 'B.B.' Two things emerged. The first was a suggestion by Smith that he should re-write his book under the title *Scouting for Boys*. The other was a concern, which both men shared, that while the Brigade served boys who came to church and were prepared to attend Bible class there was a far greater number, even at the beginning of the century, who had no connection whatever with the Church. Should not something be done for *them*?

In 1907, B.P.—he was to become known everywhere by those simple initials—took a party of some thirty boys to Brownsea Island, in Poole Harbour on the south coast. There he put into practice some of the things he had written. He saw that, given the right conditions, social differences quickly disappeared, shy boys showed unexpected signs of leadership and even those who had little to do with formal religion had a strong awareness of God.

Scouting, unplanned, had begun.

At the age of fifty-one, B.P. started a new career.

Within a few years a haphazard idea had grown into an organisation, complete with South African hats, badges for achievement (which B.P. had first used with his soldiers in India), a code of behaviour—a good turn every day—and a basic rule. This was to honour God and the King. B.P. lived in an age when patriotism was undiminished, but he soon began to make it clear to his scouts that a love for one's own country must be matched by an appreciation of other peoples' cultures and inheritance. Scouting began to 'go international' very soon after it was born.

So swift was its growth and so evident its influence for good that by 1910 a Scout Rally had been arranged at Windsor Great Park. Unhappily King Edward VII was almost dying by the time the arrangements were in hand. Yet, standing outside the bedroom door, B.P. heard the king's word of encouragement and his charge to carry on. The Rally took place and Prince George held the inspection. Finally, in 1912, the Boy Scouts were granted a royal charter.

Two wars came, and went, drenching the world with horror. But scouting lived on. Now there are over 12 million scouts, cub scouts and scouters in more than 100 member countries. The wars created hatred between the nations, but scouting remained a bond of union and understanding. Few occasions demonstrated so clearly the ideals of scouting as the World Jamboree held at Arrowe Park, in Birkenhead in 1929. There, with 56,000 scouts and scouters forming an immense wheel of friendship, each spoke consisting of thousands of boys radiating outwards from the centre, B.P. stood at the hub of the wheel. He took a hatchet and thrust it into a barrel of earth. 'Here is the hatchet of war, of bad feeling, of enmity,' he cried. 'I bury it now in Arrowe.' Then he lifted a bundle of golden arrows. As they moved back from hand to hand down the long spokes B.P. spoke again.

'Today I send you from Arrowe into all the world, bearing this symbol of peace and fellowship on the wings of sacrifice and service.

'Carry it fast and far so that all men may know the Brotherhood of Man.'

4
U Ba Ohn

OUT OF TRIBULATION

The First World War was over when Ba Ohn was born, and no more than its echoes reached the hot, dry country of central Burma. Nationalism was not yet a mood of the people, though it was already beginning to dominate Indian political thinking. Japan was scarcely a country on the map to the children of Ba Ohn's school. Communism, claiming its victims in the bloody Bolshevik revolution in Russia, left the southern countries of Asia untroubled and unaware.

To the European, Burma was remote, an oriental land of mystery. Yet within a score of years after Ba Ohn's birth it was to be trampled by British soldiers in retreat before victorious Japanese armies, and its patriots, inspired by their own interpretation of Communism, were to claim an independence that, in its isolationism, was to reject not only the West but the influence of all foreigners on its life.

In this country, dragged so swiftly into the arena of war and international politics, the Christian Church was a tiny community, made up of scattered groups, almost infinitesimal in the Buddhist-dominated south and centre of the land. On the northern borders the Welsh missionaries of Assam had influenced some of the hill tribes, but the true Burmese had little but contempt for these Shan and Lushai tribesmen who believe in a 'spirit' indwelling natural objects and happenings—'animism', as this belief is called. The unprejudiced observer would hardly have expected so tiny a group, based on an 'alien' faith, to survive the holocaust of war and the isolationism which followed it.

It was due to young men like Ba Ohn that it not only survived, but grew in numbers, maturity and effectiveness.

Ba Ohn's father was a teacher in a vernacular school in the Pokokku district. His parents were Christian though apparently without any deep sense of commitment, and the family, five sons and a daughter, were brought up in this faith. Leaving school, Ba Ohn joined his older brother at Chauk, in the service of the Burma Oil Company. Chauk was a considerable industrial centre, with Indian and Chinese workers as well as Burmese. It was about this time that the Methodist Church opened up its work there, and the Oil Company provided a building in which all denominations could meet for worship.

The conventional Christian faith of Ba Ohn's brother deepened and it was he who drew the younger man into the fellowship of the church. A small group of young men began to study the Bible in the missionary's manse after service on Sunday evenings, and before long they were not only witnessing in Chauk itself but conducting worship in outlying villages on Sundays and attempting to evangelise in the neighbourhood. How deep their faith was only time would tell.

The test came quickly.

At the end of 1941 the Japanese bombed the American fleet in Pearl Harbour and within six months were pressing home their claim to be the imperial masters of South-East Asia. On Good Friday, 1942, just after the morning services had ended, Mandalay was bombed, and the crowded wooden houses of the city went up in flames. In face of the advancing Japanese armies it was clear that the presence of European missionaries could only bring hostility and persecution to the Christian Church. For the Church's sake as well as for their own safety they were urged to leave the country.

Burmese Christians were left on their own. In the years that followed it became startlingly clear that the Spirit of God was giving them power, courage and guidance. European leadership was not indispensable to those to whom God was a living reality.

As the Japanese advanced, Ba Ohn, married to Ma Mya Khin, a Buddhist girl who had been baptised a Christian, left Chauk to cross the Irrawaddy and live in his own family area near Pakokku. Then, as the invaders established themselves and began to reactivate the oil installations which the departing British had blown up, he returned to Chauk with his brother. Here they helped to draw together a group of young Christians. Despite Japanese hostility they did not give up witnessing for Christ, to the surprise of their fellow-Burmese, and only one suffered death. They had leapt into a slit-trench to hide from bombing aircraft and, when the planes had passed, got out again, sheltering their eyes to see the planes more clearly. One young man was accused of signalling to the aircraft and taken away to die after a vicious beating-up.

'But why do you go on witnessing to this Jesus now that the Europeans have gone?' asked the Buddhists. 'Isn't Christianity a white man's religion? Isn't Jesus white? Does Christianity still exist in Burma?'

The rest of Ba Ohn's life has been given to demonstrating that Christianity is not merely a white man's religion, that Jesus is the Saviour of all men, not least of the people of Burma.

Despite some falling away under pressure from the Japanese and from Buddhist priests who co-operated with them, the Church in the main stood firm. Though they heard of persecutions, even deaths, Ba Ohn and his friends maintained their witness in Chauk.

By the time the missionaries returned after the war he was clear in his own mind that God was calling him to give full-time service to the Church. His brother was to become one of its leading laymen, and his sister a woman worker, while Ba Ohn undertook ministerial training in Mandalay with a group of other young men. This new injection of young blood was of immense importance. The small number of Burmese ministers was growing older and, in some cases, was out of touch with events.

Then came the second tribulation for the Church. Burma gained its independence and quickly expressed its hostility to Indian traders, American industrialists, British missionaries and the like by expelling all foreigners, a decisive action taking only a few months. In 1965 the last Methodist missionaries were compelled to leave. Once more the Church was on its own. In the same year the Burmese Methodist Church became autonomous, though it was still permitted to receive funds from abroad. U Ba Ohn became the first President of the Methodist Conference of Upper Burma. With a congregation of his own in Mandalay he had to travel widely and constantly throughout the three districts of the Church, as far north as the hill-country bordering Assam.

By this time the lessons of the war period had been truly learned. With God, the Church was not alone. The fellowship of prayer was maintained with those who had known and loved it, and with thousands who had never been to Burma or even out of their own country. Far more than money, this prayer-support was urged and valued. The news that came from the Church proved without any doubt that God was at work in it and through it. Young people went on evangelistic treks, distributed Christian literature at fairs and cinemas, formed their own missionary organisation. In the north the tribespeople displayed new interest in the Gospel. Shan, Kongsai, Keren, Chin and Lushai asked for the good news. House-groups found their attention being caught by the doctrines of Christian Perfection and Sanctification.

For six years U Ba Ohn travelled, guided, responded to the needs of his people before he handed over his responsibility as President to his successor. Under his leadership, out of tribulation the Church demonstrated that God gives the power to overcome to those who live by His power and witness in His name.

OVER THE WALL AT THE 'VIC'

The 'Old Vic' is one of the most famous theatres in the world, and in many ways the most notable in Britain. Its first aim was to offer the best in drama and opera to the poverty-stricken dwellers in the squalid streets round the New Cut—The area near Waterloo Station where Thomas Bowman Stephenson began the work that was to result in the National Children's Home.

The 'Vic' was successful from the beginning—and its success was founded on practicality, hard work and prayer. The genius behind it was the least likely person imaginable—a down-to-earth, cockney-voiced, plain woman who carried the aura of the Victorian era with her throughout her life—Lilian Baylis.

But the theatre did not begin with Lilian; and Lilian did not begin in Lambeth.

Child of thoroughly Bohemian parents, both talented musicians, she was taken with them to South Africa where they toured the veldt towns in a covered wagon, singing and playing the great music of the world. Lilian set up as a teacher of music in Johannesburg, and for five years was conductor of a ladies' orchestra. Then came a letter from her aunt, Emma Cons. She needed help to manage the 'Old Vic'.

Opened in 1818, the Royal Victoria Theatre had suffered the same fate as innumerable others in London, where at the end of Queen Victoria's reign there were eight music halls for every theatre. Lewd, immoral, centres of drunkenness and vice, music-halls were mostly too degraded for adults, much more the children who were dragged to them. Emma Cons took over the disreputable music-hall by the New Cut, an area avoided even by the police, reconstructed it to some extent, and opened it as a Temperance Music Hall with lantern slides, penny lectures, buns and a coffee bar. On her aunt's death in 1912 Lilian Baylis took charge, with immediate and dramatic results.

Her great love was opera, but under the pressure of her friends she began the production of Shakespeare, too, so that before long the theatre was accepted as the true centre of Shakespearean drama. Not that Lilian ever sat through the plays with an eye on either the drama or the actors—though she had an uncanny knack of being all attention when some poor actor dropped his sword or muffed his lines. True, she sat in her own box near the stage, but she occupied her time writing letters of appeal for more and more help to an endless number of friends and acquaintances. One of these close friends said that she not only wrote the sort of letters a vicar would write in seeking support for a parish-hall event, but she treated the whole of the local population like her parish.

She would never increase the prices beyond what she felt the poor people round her could pay. Her aim was simply to give these Londoners the best in music and drama because she loved them and because they deserved it. Why should they be deprived, or driven to the local music-halls, because few of them had had much schooling or much money in their pockets? When some of her 'locals' could not get into the cheap seats in the gallery, she turned well-dressed patrons out of boxes for which they had paid. She fried sausages in the wings to feed the hungriest of her young actors and actresses, who were often not much better off than the audience. She was not prepared to pay big money for big names—they should be privileged to play for next to nothing, since it was the Old Vic!

Like her local audiences, her staff adored her, not merely for what she did—though that was remarkable enough—but for what she was. Above everything else, she was an utterly dedicated Christian woman.

Such spare time as she had was often devoted to visiting the Leper Colony at St Giles, run by Anglo-Catholic sisters of mercy. Here she was loved as much as in the New Cut. Brusque and unsentimental, she took hope and faith wherever she went.

She affirmed to everyone that she believed in love and in God. It was unnecessary to add that she believed in the Old Vic, for she believed that God was as interested in it as she was herself. That was why she never found it odd to pray about every detail of her theatre's life. To Lilian, prayer was not quietness and listening, an escape from busy pressures into some quiet place. It was 'demand', and she prayed everywhere until an answer came. What was more, she expected everyone to do the same, and to have the same unshakable faith.

'I know you've all been praying about this,' was a common opening to a discussion about who was to play Hamlet or whether they could buy new scenery or whether the price of seats should eventually go up. In their book *Lilian Baylis*, Sybil and Russell Thorndike, who worked with her so long, catch her at prayer again and again. In her office, with her hand on the telephone, either by accident or as a reminder that prayer was really communication, she would begin: 'Dear God . . .' When she told a young actress who, against orders for the Vic, smoked behind the scenes, that she had been praying for her to stop smoking all day long she received a rude answer. The girl did not want praying for. Lilian's brief rejoinder was that someone had to!

She took for granted that 'prayer worked'. It had to, if God was the sort of God she believed in—caring, interested and compassionate. So

Lilian, at least, was not surprised one day when she cycled home from a ride in the country. Among the fields she had stalked into a tiny village church, said aloud that she refused to kneel since she had already knelt too often asking for an urgent sum of money without getting any answer, assured God that since no one amongst her Management Committees and her friends would do anything He must do something Himself—and that surely He didn't want the Vic to close down, did He?

When she reached her office there was a cheque on the desk for the exact amount she needed.

It was not all demand, however. She asked advice on everything, too. Should they do *Macbeth*? Should she engage this actor, or that? Should she write to this person, or not? She seldom acted until she believed the answer had come.

The theatre was the most unlikely place to find such an uncompromising, high-minded, penny-counting, unsophisticated woman as this Victorian who seemed to have strayed into the twentieth century. When she died, just before a production of *Macbeth* in 1937, a critic of much ability said that she was 'a strange woman . . . strange that a woman so ill-equipped for her task should have succeeded in doing so much.' Lilian might well have agreed. Then, no doubt, she would have turned back to one of her favourite phrases from the Psalms . . . so much more vivid than 'nothing being impossible with God':

'With the help of my God I shall leap over the wall.'

6
John Beekman

THE WAY THROUGH THE WILDERNESS

'The boy's heart has a murmur,' said the doctor. 'He'll always have to go carefully.'

John Beekman was ten years old, the son of Dutch parents living at Newark, New Jersey, twenty miles from the Hudson river. Solid, conservative folk, they belonged to the equally traditionalist and conservative Reformed Church. If a murmuring heart was God's will for the boy he would have to learn to live with it.

In 1943 John was at the Moody Bible Institute in Chicago, hoping to follow a missionary career. His heart still troubled him and he waited for the medical report with a sense of unease. The doctor saw no reason to hide things from those who were supposed to be sustained by Christian faith and fortitude.

'You may live to be forty. It's not very likely you'll live to get far past it,' said the doctor, adding that if *he* had that sort of heart-condition he would rather die amongst the Indians than rust out in a safe place.

It was the answer John wanted. There was no shallow comfort in it, but it had a trumpet-sound of courage. The problem, however, remained. What mission board would take the risk of training, equipping and sending a man like him to some remote place where medical care would be minimal? Even to a missionary society he was a bad risk. It would certainly have to be a faith mission, in every sense of the term. And there was one such society to which John Beekman's mind was turning.

'There are more than a thousand tribes which do not have a word of the Gospel in their own tongues. Most of them have languages which have never been written down.' This was the challenge to which William Cameron Townsend had responded by founding the Wycliffe Bible Translators. Beekman was not qualified as a 'translator', but they also needed literacy workers and, with his wife Elaine, he put in an application for an interview.

The doctor who examined him did not even notice his heart, and he was accepted. In 1947 he and Elaine set out for Mexico. He had been posted to the southernmost province of that country, Chiopas, which had its frontier alongside Guatemala and whose people were ninety per cent Indians, descended from the great Maya people whom the Spaniards had conquered in the sixteenth century.

Mexico sounded exotic but Amado Nervo, the village where the

Beekmans were to live, was magnificent only in its situation. The people were poor, illiterate and deprived. They had no health services, found their only relaxation in drunkenness and were more or less serfs of the powerful Spanish-speaking coffee ranchers. The Mexican government offered twenty-five-acre plots to Indians who would cultivate them, but no peasant dared take up the offer because of reprisals from the ranchers. The religion of the Chols, the tribe amongst whom the Beekmans had come to live, was a mixture of pagan superstition, Maya-derived, and the most degraded forms of mediaeval Catholicism. The devil rather than God dominated all their rites.

Where did a literacy worker begin amongst such people?

Elaine tried to adapt herself to local conditions and John began to learn the language. Before long he was wandering the mountain trails on preaching tours, his heart thumping every time he went uphill. At home his learning of the language was interrupted by people who came for medicine, to have teeth pulled, to gossip or even to watch the strange foreigners as they ate, washed or worked. Yet these, as he realised, were less interruptions than opportunities to learn the language and thought-forms of the people.

There were long periods in the years which followed when John and Elaine felt very much in the wilderness. They were opposed and cursed by the witch-doctor, and when their first child died the villagers were sure it was because of the curse he had put upon it. They were, for the most part, out of touch with colleagues. They were dogged by illness, and oppressed by isolation. There was so much to do that the little they did achieve seemed scarcely to bite into the edge of the Chol problems.

Yet, at the end of four years, John had a team of boy-preachers some fifty strong whom he trained each week and who went on preaching tours through the hill villages every weekend. He had begun work on a Spanish-Chol dictionary. The witch-doctor was dead, after a drunken brawl. The little church was filled every Sunday.

More important than any of these things, in the long run, he had realised that literacy work was of little use if people had nothing to read. He had begun work on translating the New Testament into Chol.

Five years after they had reached Amado Nervo the first draft of the translation was finished. It was, however, very much a first rough working-copy. The help of other workers, from other Chol-speaking areas, was essential. As a result a very significant conference was held for five weeks. At the end not only had an immense amount of work been done on the translation but John Beekman saw two things very clearly. The first was that literal translation was not only inadequate but often quite misleading. Phrases must be translated into the idiom, into the social background, of new readers. And, judging by the work achieved by the group, 'translators' workshops' were essential if the task of getting the gospel into the world's tribal tongues by the end of the century was to be accomplished. He started to work harder than ever, his time shortened by medical clinics, dentistry, pastoral work, preachers' classes and preaching tours.

Then, in 1955, with the translation nearly ready for the printer, John's heart almost stopped completely. He was still four years short of the forty he had been given.

In Mexico City one of the world's most delicate operations was performed. 'One chance in two that you'll live—or die,' said the doctor. There were two of them having the same operation that week. One man died. John, supported by a battery of prayer and his own determination to carry out what he had begun, recovered.

Four years later, just after Easter, the Chol translation arrived from the American Bible Society.

John held the red-bound book in his hands and gave thanks for what the Gospel had achieved amongst the Chols. Churches were being built, and filled. Old opponents had been won for the Christian faith. There was food in the houses, shoes on children's feet and the light of health in their eyes. The tribespeople had courageously taken up the government's offer of land and were becoming self-sufficient instead of being the serfs of the ranchers.

Yet more than this had happened. A splendid new centre for 'Translators' Workshops' was built. John Beekman himself, after a period away from Mexico acting as director of the Wycliffe team in Guatemala, had been appointed Translation Co-ordinator for Wycliffe translators all over the world. In his 1967 report he noted that 327 translators working in 231 languages had received consultative help. The time for producing a translation into a tribal tongue was being cut by half.

Despite having the heart of a man of eighty, John Beekman, fifty years old, could still sing:

> 'My Lord knows the way through the wilderness,
> And all I have to do is follow.'

7

Folke Bernadotte

'SERVE ONLY HONOUR'

In 1922 a tall, slim, splendidly-dressed cavalry officer received from King Gustav the gold medal for the best officer in the Swedish army. At the age of twenty-seven it was the second time he had won this coveted prize. But this time it was the end of an era. For Folke Bernadotte it also seemed the end of all he loved best in life.

Count Bernadotte was the king's nephew. In a highly democratic country he had gone to an ordinary school and mixed with ordinary people, but unlike most of them he had no real need to work for a living, and was able to choose precisely the way of life which suited him. For Bernadotte there had never been any real choice. Life, for him, had always been horses. At the age of twenty he was an ensign in the King's Lifeguards. Now, with the gold medal in his hand, depression swept over him. The Swedish army—which, in a neutral country, had never seen active service—was being mechanised.

The king asked him, in view of this change, what he would like to do.

His answer was very brief. 'Nothing!'

For the next ten years that was more or less what he did.

He took his turn on guard at the palace as a member of the royal bodyguard. He went to parties and travelled. He drifted through an aimless social existence, bored and unimaginative.

'A dull fellow,' commented the king, when Bernadotte accompanied him on holiday to the French Riviera and Monte Carlo. 'Thirty-three and not even married.' But it was on this very holiday that the yacht of an American millionaire swept into the harbour. Its owner was invited to dine with the king, and Bernadotte met Estelle Manville, the millionaire's daughter. Within a few months they were engaged and the following year they were married.

Though he did not know it Count Folke Bernadotte's aimless existence had come to an end.

Estelle was charming, intelligent, gifted, and determined that her husband should begin to contribute something to life. He found himself—to his own surprise—working in an American bank, then in a business house, and then learning French to become a bank clerk in France!

He developed interests outside the commercial world, too. During a stroll with a friend he saw a great gathering of Boy Scouts and went to see what it was all about. At that moment his cousin, Crown Prince

Olav, drove up to inspect the rally and invited Bernadotte to share the inspection with him. It was not long before he himself was in the youth movement which, in Sweden, included the Y.M.C.A., the Salvation Army and the Good Templars. Within a year or so he had visited every scout centre between the Baltic and the Arctic Circle.

In 1939 he went to the United States, visiting Swedish communities and organising the Swedish pavilion at the New York World Fair. It was while he was there that tragedy struck in Europe. News came that Nazi Germany and Russia had signed a pact of friendship. Then, on 1st September, the world heard that Russia and Germany had invaded Poland.

The Second World War had begun.

In neutral Sweden peace reigned, uneasily. Bernadotte would have found no difficulty in evading the effects of war, or any involvement in it. Instead he quickly made links with the Red Cross. After overseeing some of the internment camps in Sweden itself his first task was to visit Germany, where in 1940, he persuaded the Nazi government to agree to an exchange of a few hundred seriously-ill prisoners-of-war between Germany and Britain. It was the first and last gesture of this kind.

Neutral though he was, he did not escape danger. Two years later he flew to Berlin, nearly crashing on the way in heavy fog. In the city he was followed by spies and Gestapo members and was in the Swedish embassy when it was destroyed by British bombs. Flying to Britain in the bomb-bay of a Mosquito aircraft he narrowly escaped disaster and, in London had to shelter from German air-attacks. But these, to Count Bernadotte, were the inescapable hazards of a Red Cross worker involved in trying to ease the conditions of prisoners-of-war. As the years went by he penetrated the concentration camps—Neuegamme, for instance, from which he arranged the repatriation of Scandinavian resistance workers, and the dreaded Ravensbruck, where he was the first Red Cross officer to see the horrors which pressmen later described to the world.

Before the war ended he had been responsible for saving from the prison camps over 30,000 prisoners from thirty nations. After it was over the task facing the Red Cross was immeasurably greater. With some thirty million refugees in Europe, thirteen million of them children, the task was superhuman. Bernadotte travelled throughout Germany; inspected welfare work in Holland, Belgium and Poland; gave assistance to Finland; went on missions to all the Baltic countries; traversed the bandit-infested hills of Greece to help Queen Frederika in her own work of rehabilitation.

Only occasionally did he see anything of his home in Stockholm. It was there, however, the scene of his earlier life as an aristocratic playboy, that he received his last and most demanding commission.

On 21st May, 1948, he had a telegram from Trygve Lie, the Secretary-General of the United Nations, informing him that the U.N. wished him to leave at once for Palestine to act as mediator between Jews and Arabs in the bitter conflict which had then broken out.

Four days after he received the request he set off for the Mediterranean, setting up his headquarters in Rhodes. In a fortnight he flew seven thousand miles round the Middle Eastern capitals, persuaded the combatants to agree to a four-week truce, and returned to New York to report to the U.N. In the two months that followed, his white plane was constantly in and out of Israel and Jordan. Anonymous letters threatening his life reached him in Rhodes. More threats arrived at his home when he was presiding over the Red Cross Conference in Stockholm. On his return to Jerusalem a radio message reached the pilot that there would be an attempt on Bernadotte's life. He asked the Count what he should do.

'Fly on!' ordered Bernadotte.

The next day an amateur radio operator in Sweden picked up the message that shocked the world.

'Folke Bernadotte shot today, 17th September, in Jerusalem. Death instantaneous.'

The motto of the Swedish king's lifeguards was: *Serve Only Honour.* None of its officers held it more dear than Count Folke Bernadotte. But he served more than honour. He served humanity.

In Rhodes, just before he left on his last tragic flight, he opened a parcel with care, thinking it might contain a bomb. Instead it held a new Bible, a present from his father. His old one had fallen to pieces from constant use and he had had no time to buy another in Stockholm.

Honour. Humanity. Both of these he served. But, above all, he served God.

8
Edith Brown

MISS BROWN'S HOSPITAL

That was how the Indian people of the Punjab described it and, indeed, how thousands of supporters in Britain thought of it. Ludhiana Christian Medical College is its proper title, but it took a very long time to achieve the universal recognition which lies behind that name. It would never have been there at all, except in a very rudimentary way, if it had not been for Edith Brown.

A convinced evangelical Christian, coming from Huguenot forbears, Edith began her pioneering early. In 1881 she was one of the first group of science students at Girton College, Cambridge, in a day when even those women who passed their examinations might not have their names printed in the results-lists. Deciding to become a doctor, she studied at the Royal Free Hospital School and the London Hospital, though again she could not actually gain a degree—they were not awarded to women. Undefeated, she took a diploma in Edinburgh and a degree in Brussels. Inspired by the thought of a half-sister married to a missionary in India and convinced that God could use her to bring hope to India's millions of women, she sailed for Bombay in 1891 as a missionary of the Baptist Zenana Mission.

Ludhiana, a historic city of the Punjab, was to be her home for almost sixty years, before she retired to live out the rest of her life in Kashmir.

Appalled by the poverty and superstition she found, she might well have been disheartened by the tiny and unavailing efforts made to deal with it by the little group of Baptist women. Instead, her mind leapt to the future—to what might one day be accomplished. It was clear the needs of India's women could not be met from a base hospital, however well-equipped it might eventually become. What was wanted was a training centre which would send out women of ability, standing and Christian faith who could meet need where it existed most blatantly, in the bazaars and the villages. Even a few trained assistants would have enabled her to conduct clinics in the nearby villages, but no such assistants existed.

Meanwhile, Edith had to learn the language, come to terms with social conditions, religious attitudes and ignorance, and do what doctoring she could. Her first operation was spectacular. In a small room, with a missionary hiding her eyes and dropping chloroform on to a pad, and a Bible-woman shrieking in astonishment as she handed her

34

what was necessary, she removed an immense ovarian cyst. From that moment her legend in the bazaars was secure.

Transferred to Palwal, near Delhi, she saw at first-hand what village life involved in misery and hazard. The vision of a training institution grew more clear. Two years after her arrival in India, brash by any standards but full of faith, she had called together fourteen representatives of missionary societies working in North India and put her plan to them. Other types of missionaries might have been more hesitant, but these were doctors facing the same limitations as the newcomer. They caught something of her hopes, consulted with their home boards and, by 1894, the North India School of Medicine for Christian Women was a fact of life in Ludhiana.

The school had one full-time member of staff, Edith Brown, three part-timers, six students and a promise of £50 from a personal friend in Britain for the next few years.

At the end of five years the first group of students passed their examinations in Lahore as Hospital Assistants, and more were on the way. It was a small drop in an ocean of need, but it was a beginning.

Meanwhile Edith continued to do more than a full day's work, month after month, year after year. Long before, on going to Cambridge, she had been told by a doctor concerned for her health that she must not study after 8.30 p.m. She kept the rule, but rose at 4.0 a.m. instead! The early discipline enabled her to go on when others might have dropped out, though she herself would have said quite simply that God gave strength to those who needed it. It was not only young men who could walk and not faint, sustained by prayer, faith and the need to accomplish more than a lifetime's work in a short time. The hospital grew larger; the training school gained in reputation as its 'graduates' moved out into their life's work. Edith herself continued to operate, to run committees, to appeal for money, to wear herself out on furlough even more vigorously than she did in Ludhiana itself.

She began a scheme for training the Indian midwives—outcaste women with little knowledge, whose dirty hands and prodding sticks caused appalling injuries. After sending a crier through the bazaar to summon them she found only one woman, and she had come out of curiosity. An open manner, a friendly talk and the gift of an anna or so—'we pay money for this class; we don't take it!'—the classes increased. Possibly their most significant feature was the trust that came to exist between the British surgeon and this group of ignorant women, whom every other European seemed to despise.

There was never really enough money, though every year closed without debt. There were never really enough workers, though Christian women made applications in excess of the number of students who could be taken. But by 1906 the Punjab Government was making grants and, in 1915, closed the Lahore Medical College so that students might come instead to Ludhiana. By that time both the name and the constitution had changed so that non-Christian women might also be accepted. It had become the Women's Christian Medical College. To Edith, though she made explicit demands about the orthodoxy of her staff, it was good that Hindus and Sikhs as well as Christians should learn to serve their own people. She saw her role, as she said, as 'the voice of a stranger', but she saw, too, a day when an army of Christian women would fight ignorance 'as only those belonging to the people can'. If some of those who came were not Christians it was good that they should see Christianity at close quarters. As a result some, though not all, found a Saviour as well as a new role in life.

Year by year the changes came. By the beginning of the Second World War the college and hospital covered fifteen acres. By 1945 ex-students were serving with twenty-seven missionary societies throughout India. Edith Brown had been twice decorated by the Indian Government and made a Dame Commander of the British Empire. In 1942 she handed over to her successor the Hospital and College she had created fifty years earlier.

Then, sixty years after Edith arrived in India, Ludhiana achieved University status; her dream had come true. Her college was able to grant M.B. and B.S. degrees. At last it was producing fully-qualified doctors.

From Kashmir, where she retired to a delightful houseboat on the Dal Lake, Dame Edith was still involved in evangelism—opening a Christian reading room, running Bible correspondence courses, using new Gospel recordings. But it was Ludhiana which held her heart. Ludhiana—with its 12,000 in-patients and 90,000 out-patients; its seventy doctors and 150 nurses; its almost endless departments—radiology, psychiatry, tuberculosis, pediatrics, dentistry, amongst others. Ludhiana, still truly a Christian Medical College.

Few women missionaries had seen so many of their dreams come true, even at the age of ninety-two.

ARCHBISHOP OF THE POOR WORLD

Recife, metropolis of north-east Brazil, has a million inhabitants, most of them poor, the majority desperately so. Until 1964 it was little known outside South America, and even today most people in Europe would not know what country it is in. That it has leapt into the conscience of concerned men and women is due to its archbishop. His name is both hated and venerated. He himself is traduced as a Communist, a renegade Christian, and loved as a saint.

Helder Camara has been Archbishop of Olinda and Recife since April, 1964, when the new see was created at the instance of the Pope.

A visiting journalist was taken aback when he asked the way to the archbishop's palace. His informant just laughed at the question.

'Follow the first poor man, and you're likely to get there.'

Nearer the palace he did indeed follow a poor man, and a disturbed woman talking incoherently to herself. In the poor world of Recife the 'palace' need have been no surprise, except that it was the outward symbol of the dominant faith, a Catholic Church identified through the centuries in Latin America with power, prestige, wealth and domination.

Helder Camara, in his mid-fifties when he was appointed archbishop, lives in a small house with two rooms, sparsely furnished. One has a sort of hammock in which he sleeps—for fours hours a night. He regards the hammock and the sleep as luxury enough for a busy man. Short, pale, bald, with a lined face, he wears a creased black cassock and a wooden cross on an iron chain. When he is in Recife—and he is away from it a good deal—one of the rooms acts as a waiting room and is normally full of people, most of them poor.

He has become the apostle of the poor, nor merely of Brazil or of Latin America, but of the world.

His upbringing seemed unlikely to endear the Church to him. Born in north-east Brazil, to which he has now returned, his father was a merchant, something of a journalist, and an atheistic freemason. His mother went to church only once a year, at a time of festival. His five brothers died young, of dysentery and lack of proper care. Even merchants had not enough money for medicine, and hospital attention was almost non-existent around the beginning of the century.

Despite this unlikely atmosphere, young Helder knew at the age of eight that he must be a priest. His vocation was encouraged by the

Church and in his training he was taught not to question its history, its beliefs or its decisions. He absorbed its attitudes—those of a Church which since the days of Spanish colonisation had been on the side of privilege and authority, which had not only been a supporter of the government but had made the governments themselves. It was not unnatural that he should have accepted its dictum that Communism was the chief evil in the world. In his own terms, be became a 'fascist'. The stage lasted until he was about twenty-six. Then he began to think for himself. There was, in him, an innate understanding of the unprivileged, but his compassion took a long time to burst the bounds of discretion.

In 1952 he was consecrated a bishop, becoming bishop-auxiliary to the Cardinal of Rio de Janeiro, and secretary of the Brazilian Episcopal Conference. Then, eight years later, in the Church of la Candelaria, he suddenly started preaching about justice. Justice for the poor; justice which expressed itself in more than 'sandwiches for a hungry man'; justice which had its roots in the teaching of Christ in the New Testament. The majority of Brazilians are illiterate and the Church did not encourage the reading of the Bible. Yet when the authentic voice of Christ is heard its accents are quickly recognised.

From that time forward Camara was a marked man—marked by the Pope as one who expressed the new concern of the Vatican for peace, justice and development; marked by the masses as one who spoke their own thoughts; marked by government, industrialists and the true fascists as a danger, to be silenced and if necessary eliminated. His appointment to Recife was regarded as almost a declaration of war between the privileged, inside and outside the Church, and the dangerous radical elements which seemed to be creeping into the Catholic church.

His first published address after his appointment included a number of statements which were dramatic in the extreme. Indeed, they were almost unbelievable to those who knew the Catholic history in Latin America. 'The bishop belongs to all' . . . 'his chief concern must be for the poor' . . . 'pioneering is the way to development' . . . 'the Church is not marginal to history; it lives at the heart of things through free, mature and responsible laity' . . . 'it would be scandalous if the Church deserted the masses' . . . 'let us liberate, in the fullest sense of the term, every human creature in our midst' . . . 'we must begin a crescendo of dialogue between rich and poor, management and workers, left and right, believer and unbeliever' . . .'what virtue is there in venerating pretty images of Christ if we do not see His face in every Jose, Antonio and Severino amongst the people?' . . . 'the Church must not merely spend time in trying to reform others; it must reform itself!'

If these were strange words from a new archbishop, they were followed by yet stronger ones.

He condemned the government for its policy of terrorism. In Paris—he speaks French fluently—the Sports Palace was filled as he denounced, in terrible detail, the torture procedures used by the Brazilian government to keep itself in power and its enemies in subjection. What he said abroad he had no fear in repeating at home, Churchmen of all kinds began to see him as a prophet who matched words with deeds.

Poverty is endemic in the sprawling city of Recife. The gap between rich and poor seems unbridgeable. In splendid houses and luxurious flats live the wealthy; in shanty towns sprawl the poor; squalid, dying too easily and early, almost without a home. At the delta of the Beberibe and Capabariba rivers families squelch in the mud, building a little wall when the tide is out, raising the walls a little every time it recedes again. They live practically in the water. Because no new building is permitted the squatters put up some bamboo poles in a shanty area and fling a few mats over them to make a roof, all in the dark hours of one night, hoping the police will not see that a new 'house' has been built.

'Justice means the right to decent housing,' asserts Camara, 'the right to work, to just wages, to political freedom.' Yet, though he defies the government, alienates many of his own Church, identifies himself with the unprivileged, he still rejects violence as the way to settle disputes. The violence of the rich must not be answered by the violence of the poor. The only way to true development is to make men conscious of the need for justice. The non-violent revolution may seem impossible, but it is the only way to hope and peace.

To the right-wing defenders of Latin American dictatorships Camara ranks with the Communists. They assert that he is a communist in priest's clothing. Camara retorts that he agrees with the communist ideals of justice, but rejects their methods and their philosophy of life and history. He remains, utterly and irrevocably, a Christian. His denials carry little weight with his enemies—and he has plenty. Communism, and Camara's interpretation of Christianity as 'rights for the poor', are equally destructive of dictatorial power in the hands of the few. The governing elite will not forego their privileges. The industrialist regards men as factory-fodder; the poorer they are the more content they will be to work for low wages.

Camara tours the world. He may be in Berlin or Moscow one week, and in Osaka or Rome the next. His words bring hope to the under-developed world of Africa, Asia and Latin America, where eighty per cent of the world's population shares twenty per cent of its wealth. In these places he is not only welcome but safe. At home, he is a man contended over, and always in danger. There are threatening letters, anonymous telephone calls, and it does not stop there. In his own church machine-gun bullets spattered the walls but did not reach him. His home was attacked and the gunmen narrowly missed killing him. In the first case a student friend was maimed for life, in the other a friend was dragged away, hanged in chains and shot to death. Camara knows the bullets may not always miss their real target.

Yet he remains serene; angry only at injustice and poverty, hunger and men's lack of true freedom. The source of his anger and his serenity are plainly stated, again and again. They lie deeper than the quotations from the New Testament. They are more intimate than the worship of a historical person who once gave Himself to the poor of Palestine.

'To me,' Camara says simply, 'Christ is not an abstract idea. He is a personal friend.'

10
Leonard Cheshire

AFTER THE BOMB DROPPED

It was 9th August, 1945.

In the B-29 which had taken off from Tinian, the tiny coral island in the Pacific, in the early hours of the morning, sat two Englishmen. One was a scientist, a mathematician of exceptional brilliance, William Penney; the other a much-decorated R.A.F. officer, Leonard Cheshire. The only non-Americans in the aircraft, they were official observers of the dropping of the second atomic bomb on Japan. When the blast had almost obliterated Nagasaki and the mushroom cloud rose two miles into the sky, Cheshire felt an excitement such as he had seldom known even on his own fantastic bombing missions.

This, he believed, was not only the end of the Japanese war. It was the end of war itself—provided Britain, with the United States, held this ultimate sanction of atomic death. He saw his career in the Royal Air Force at an end and a completely new one beginning.

At Buckingham Palace he received his decorations from King George VI—the Victoria Cross and a second bar to his D.S.O. He already held the D.F.C. The King asked what he was going to do next.

'I am going in for scientific research,' he answered. In his own imagination he already saw himself successful, a name in the headlines and in scientific circles. Cheshire never lacked a colossal self-confidence. He had no need of God, even if God existed—which he doubted—and, whenever he set his hand to a scheme, he seldom felt that he needed the guidance of others. Even if most of his ideas were momentary enthusiasms he had no doubt that he could carry them through.

There was plenty in the past to justify his belief in himself.

He had been a born leader at his public school, Stowe, and at Oxford. He liked excitement, limelight, money and all it could buy. The outbreak of war in 1939 seemed to offer fulfilment to his ebullient temperament, and flying the most dangerous and exuberant kind of life. Discipline irked him and he regarded regulations as something to be tested and not infrequently broken—whether it was by flying when he had been ordered not to do so, or by taking 'other ranks' into establishments reserved for officers. He had no fear of those in authority though he respected them when he felt that they were right. He did not always think so—and life then became difficult for both parties. His own authority, when he came to command, was based entirely on his

41

personal qualities. He dismissed his first parade on his new station with the command: 'You can go now!' Within days he had built up his own legend on the station and gained a respect denied to more efficient administrators.

His personal role was that of bomber pilot, and his aim was to establish a system of completely accurate bombing. In this he had two intentions. The first was to do the utmost damage to the selected target, and at the same time to boost the morale of his own crew by doing so. The second was to cause as little damage to non-military targets as possible. This was demonstrated on one of the first 'pin-point' bomb attacks in his career, on Limoges in France.

The target was an undefended aero-engine plant established by the Nazis. He flew in very low, and his approach gave warning of the coming attack. There were no bombs. He flew in again as the factory-girls began to stream out and dash for the shelters. Not until he believed the workers were all in safety did he call in his bombing-fleet for the third time to devastate the factory.

It was Cheshire's 'pin-point' theory of bombing that gained him his name and reputation. It was the courage he displayed in following it out that won him such repeated military decorations.

Peacetime conditions, for such a man, held both frustration and challenge. Back in civilian life at the end of the war he bought a large house in Kensington, put down a deposit on a new Bentley, and set himself up with new suits from an exclusive Mayfair tailor.. Slight in figure, black-haired, brown-eyed, intense in pleasure or planning new schemes, he was a vivid personality ready to respond to exploitation of himself in the popular press. He wrote articles, toured the country lecturing about the need for atomic supremacy, found time for gay parties and night club life . . . and wondered why he was impatient, uneasy and frustrated. With seemingly endless resources of energy and ideas he was looking for a purpose in life . . . indeed, looking for a cause. He could not find one.

Certainly such a purpose would have no relation to religious belief. In a night club he insisted that God was a product of our own imagination—and was taken aback when a girl in the party turned on him in angry astonishment and declared her own Christian faith.

Slowly he realised that there were many other ex-servicemen with his views about the peace. Old jobs were unattractive, new ones difficult to find. Why not a colony of ex-servicemen working together? So 'V.I.P.' was born—'Very Important Persons'—in a large house and grounds in Market Harborough. They would grow flowers for market, breed rabbits for sale as food and mice for sale as pets. But horticulture is a tricky trade, and not enough people wanted rabbits and mice. The situation was poor. The colony was riven by problems of temperament.

Even so, Cheshire did not give up. Instead, he found a large house in Hampshire, and in 1947 V.I.P. moved to Le Court.

By now the seeds of failure were already coming to harvest. Cheshire spent time on the continent, and in recuperating from over-work and stress in Canada. His earlier dismissal of religion was less assured and in Canada he came close to the beginnings of certainty. God was no longer remote.

When he got back to Hampshire, recalled by an urgent telegram, he discovered that Le Court had almost ground to a final halt. The ex-servicemen were working elsewhere or preparing to leave. Partly it was the absence of Cheshire's own magnetism, partly the fallacy of the original idea that because men had fought in the same war they would live and work together amicably in the days of peace. He prepared to close down, for there seemed nothing else to do.

It was then that he went to hospital to see Arthur Dykes, an old resident of the home whom he found dying of cancer and without home or friends. He was taking up a wanted bed in hospital, but there was no place to which he might be discharged.

Cheshire took him 'home' to Le Court.

Almost immediately he was under attack. 'An adventurer . . . a charlatan . . . a one-man nursing-home . . . no medical skill . . . hare-brained and egotistical.' Cheshire took little notice. All he wanted to do at that moment was to comfort a dying man and give him the security of affection. This he did. His smart suits had been discarded for old flannels and a blue battle-dress jacket. His innate compassion, manifested when he bombed Limoges, had full play. But though Dykes needed love he had another source of security. He was a devout Christian, a Catholic, dying in peace.

More than anyone else Arthur Dykes, dying of cancer, brought Cheshire to the end of his spiritual pilgrimage. Not all his questions were answered, but of God he no longer had any doubt. Nor, indeed, did he doubt that with his new sense of faith God had shown him the purpose of his life.

Arthur Dykes, too, had decided the way forward for Le Court. No longer would it be a home for the healthy, but for the ex-prisoner or the mentally unstable. It should be for those who had no hope of recovery. In time, because of the pressure of many in need, there were new limitations, deliberately self-imposed by Cheshire and his colleagues. But for two years this Hampshire house was the only centre for a work which Cheshire began to see must develop much more widely.

Visiting Culdrose, the Fleet Air Arm's station on the Lizard peninsula in Cornwall, Cheshire found an unused air-field with a few Nissen huts going to ruin. In 1950 it became his second 'Home'. Now there could be no turning back. He knew that God was behind all his planning, for serenity had come with his reception into the Catholic Church in 1950.

By 1954 other groups had been stimulated to begin homes of the same kind in Kent, Sussex and Bedfordshire. Quickly the concern spread to the north of England and to Scotland. In 1955 Cheshire was invited to Bombay, to advise on possibilities there, and himself took over a small asbestos hut, without lights or water, outside the city. It was the beginning of a wide outreach overseas. Today there are more than fifty homes in the United Kingdom and as many overseas in places as widespread as Chile and Ceylon, Portugal and the Philippines, Thailand and the Middle East. Designed now for the permanently handicapped, apart from one or two for children and for adult rehabilitation, they are centres of self-help where residents learn to use their skills to the full, both for their own enjoyment and the service of the community. They do, indeed, become a real part of the community. Though they receive a great deal of help from Rotary, Round Table and many other groups, and especially from young people, they often seem to contribute as much as they give.

Cheshire has known joy and anxiety since the Homes started. For a time he was seriously ill with tuberculosis and still suffers from its effects. In 1959 he married Sue Ryder, a war-time heroine whose own organisation was serving war-prisoners—'the forgotten allies'. To-gether they have begun an informal association, the 'Mission for the Relief of Suffering', which includes Mother Theresa's Missionaries of Charity. Through it Leonard Cheshire and Sue Ryder are linked with men and women of every race and many churches and religions who are committed to serve suffering humanity—that same humanity which Cheshire himself saw hurled into annihilation as he watched the Nagasaki bomb explode.

11

Walter Robert Corti

CHILDREN'S VILLAGE

Dr Corti did not want to recover. In a sanatorium at Davos, on the 'magic mountain' where tuberculosis sufferers regained their health, he seemed to the nurses the only patient who did not really care whether he lived or died. They urged him towards the will to live. Whether his chosen career were finished or not there were many other things that a man of his intellectual ability could still do. The world was still there, outside.

That, indeed, was the heart of Corti's trouble. The world was there—and he thought it a sick, indeed a mad world.

Son of a scientist from the Ticino, Italian-speaking Switzerland, he had set out, almost inevitably it seemed, on a medical career. He was a brilliant student, and followed his normal medical courses with post-graduate studies in other countries. Brain surgery was to be his field. Then, with terrible suddenness, he discovered that he had tuberculosis. Towards the beginning of the war he was sent to Davos.

In this isolated beauty spot, with his own country ringed round by warring nations, his thoughts ranged the world. War was being waged with utter ruthlessness—towns smashed out of existence, populations deported, communities exterminated. When at last it ended, how could one live in such a world of past hatreds and bitter memories? There was nothing to make a man want to get well.

The worst thought of all was the children. Orphaned, stealing and lying in order to stay alive, searching for parents already dead in concentration camps, born in states which no longer existed . . . how many children were there like this on the roads of Europe? Post-war statistics would give the number as thirteen million. With such a background, how could the children inheriting the future ever learn to live together? Unless . . . Corti began to see a reason for recovery!

'We are going to build a children's village,' said Dr Corti to the nurses. He placed an empty tobacco-tin on his bedside table. When he asked for contributions they encouraged his dream and his return to health by putting a coin in it. Wild schemes were often the sign of returning hope—though this was wild, indeed.

In August 1944 Corti wrote an article for the Swiss magazine *Du*. He was later to become its editor. Swiss people had already taken 200,000 children into their homes for short periods of convalescence. They believed in practical compassion. As a thank-offering for safety throughout two world wars Corti suggested that they should build an international children's village when the war at last ended.

Two things quickly happened. The first was that Corti was declared symptom-free, and discharged. The other was an astonishing and spontaneous response to his article. Now able to return to normal life, he devoted himself to creating reality out of his dream. There were difficulties in plenty, but they were far outweighed by the response that came from every part of the community.

Offers of land came from many parts of the country, and eventually a site was chosen, some two thousand feet high, at Trogen, in the Appenzell. The next need was money. The first four houses, typical Appenzell-type chalets, were paid for with money raised by Swiss children themselves. Then each was sold—to the towns of Zurich, Basel and Winterthur, and the chemical firm of CIBA—who each paid 793.75 Swiss francs for them, and then gave them back. Hans Fischli, a famous Swiss architect, designed the houses and the layout of the new village, personally supervising the building. This began in 1946 and the work was done by six hundred volunteers from seventeen nations.

At the end of that year the first children began to arrive—first from France, then Poles, Austrians, Hungarians, Germans, Italians, Finns and Greeks; children who had not only suffered from war, but were still marked by it in mind and attitude. Children who had been taught to regard each other as enemies for ever. Was it possible that such children could live together in understanding and peace?

It was here that the genius of Corti's plan was manifest. He had no intention of creating a mere orphanage of jumbled nationalities who must somehow learn each others' ways and languages. This was a long-term educational experiment, aimed at helping one nation to accept and explore and eventually share the culture and heritage of others. There were three criteria for children who came—and it was never intended that the numbers should be overwhelmingly large. They must be war orphans; they must be basically healthy; and they must be reasonably intelligent. These last two points were necessary if they were to be a creative community.

Pestalozzi—the village was named after the greatest of Swiss educationalists and child-humanitarians—was the only truly international children's village in Europe. Its pattern of life was that each national community had its own house, with national foster-parents, teachers and helpers. They followed their national traditions, spoke their own language, followed their own primary educational courses. At home, there was security.

In the community, at first, there were all the expected problems. German and French children, Italians and Austrians, so recently enemies, found it difficult to live as neighbours without wanting to continue the old war. Yet the enmities died more quickly than anyone imagined possible. Bonds were forged in common activities, outdoors and in the old barn which served as a community centre. They learned each other's languages by using them. When Polish and Hungarian children were withdrawn by their governments there was a shared sense of loss. When British children arrived at their new houses they came into a real community already created, as did the Tibetan children who were welcomed after the trek from Tibet which followed the Chinese invasion.

Religion has always been a natural part of the village life, and house-parents have been chosen with this in mind.

Now, with the generation of war-orphans long past, the village continues to build not a multi-racial community but a community of different nationalities sharing their cultures, their faith and their future. It is no longer a village on trial, an experiment which may or may not succeed. It is a village which has proved its value, and the faith of its founder, as its children have gone back to the lands of which they have remained citizens throughout their stay.

Dr Corti, writer, philosopher and educationist, walked in the steps of a great Swiss of an earlier generation, Henri Dunant, founder of the Red Cross, in leading his country to offer to the world a true internationalism. 'Wars are prepared and started by men,' wrote Dr Corti. 'Peace must start with the child.'

12
Julia Davis

OPERATION FRIENDSHIP

That is the name of an organisation famous thoughout Jamaica and
known widely outside that lovely island; but it might well be the
description of all Sister Julia's self-giving ministry. If she has had a
remarkable measure of success in transforming lives and situations it
has been by the power of friendship more than any other quality.

In this tall, slim, West Indian Methodist deaconess there burns a
flame of love which at times has threatened to devour her, so
unflinchingly does she give herself to those about her. Not that she is
solemn, by any means. Her eyes can flash with laughter as easily as
with indignation, and she is far more likely to burst into peals of
laughter than to shout in anger.

She did not feel like laughing the first time she went 'Back o' Wall'
in Kingston's dangerous, poverty-ridden west end. Indeed, she had
been forbidden to attempt to penetrate that terrible shanty-town for fear
of what might happen to her. But she went—and the flash in her eyes
then was affronted indignation that men and women were allowed to
live in such squalor. Not fear, but anger—until she saw the children.

That was when Operation Friendship really began, bringing new
hope to the people of Western Kingston.

It was in Western Kingston—though not in that appalling slum—that
Julia Davis herself had begun her life. She had little to boast of in her
early years, and like many of Jamaica's town-dwellers, before industry
and tourism brought new vigour to the island's economy, she knew
poverty at first hand. With her mother and sister she belonged to the
Salvation Army, but it was in a Methodist Church that she was
converted at the age of fifteen. The Church began to make a difference
to her life and some slight opportunity opened out for her. She was able
to attend the first course in social science ever run at Deaconess House,
and quickly showed her gift for dealing with small children. Helping in
the play centre she was paid ten shillings a week, and one of the
deaconesses discovered she had a gift for music as well as children.
Soon Julia was paying out a quarter of her week's wages for piano
lessons.

Outside Kingston, at Ulster Springs, the church opened a welfare
centre and Julia was given charge of the play centre. In this rural area
she trudged up the mountains, visiting people in their tiny homes. Once,
it was said, she climbed the mountains barefooted because she had

given away her shoes. The trouble with Julia, said her best friends, was that she would give away anything she possessed. Those who saw deeper still knew that, having committed herself in faith to Christ, she would always be ready to give not only her possessions but herself.

Unsophisticated, with a down-town background, Julia was accepted for training as a deaconess in a Church whose leaders were drawn from a middle-class society. With no educational advantages she attended classes at the theological college which was part of the University—and earned the reputation of having a more original mind than most students. This 'originality', really a refusal to accept conventional answers or to remain within accepted boundaries, emerged in all its dramatic effectiveness when she was stationed at Ebenezer church in 1958. Not that Julia herself appeared in any way dramatic. Quiet, rather shy, always gentle, she must have seemed the least likely person to walk deliberately into danger. That, however, in its most literal sense, is what she did.

'Back o' Wall' was the most disreputable district in a slum area whose whole reputation was shocking. It abutted onto Ebenezer church and Julia was told in the most explicit terms not to go into it. From the upper windows of the church schoolroom she could see why. Western Kingston's 150,000 residents lived in hovels of cardboard and beaten-out tin cans gone rusty. Few of these 'houses' were more than seven feet square. They had bare earth for floors and flattened cardboard cartons for beds. Between the massive, close-packed clutter of hovels she could see narrow alleys with unkempt figures jostling each other.

Julia asked God what she should do. She knew the answer before she put her prayer into words. Disobeying official instructions and commonsense, she left the church building and began to penetrate a little way into the humid, filthy, evil-smelling slum. At once it seemed as if every movement around her ceased. She was surrounded by silence, hostile and threatening.

Julia walked out of 'Back o' Wall' safely but more aware of the problems in trying to serve or meet with these people. There was no immediate break-through in the weeks that followed, but she saw the people's situation more clearly. One pit latrine shared by two hundred people; one water tap for perhaps two thousand; hungry children searching garbage piles for scraps. Theft, violence, open crime and prostitution were often the sole means of support for families unemployed for as long as they could remember. The prosperity affecting much of Jamaica from tourism and industry did not reach down to this level. Apathy, misery and despair were the key-notes of life, such as it was.

The first break came with the children, especially the tiny ones. Where everyone stood aside, suspicious and bitter, the children began to respond to Julia's evident love for them. From a tiny play-group, almost unorganised, grew a relationship with the children's mothers. They could recognise love when they saw it. Bridges began to be built.

By 1961 Operation Friendship was a reality. Protestant and Catholic churches came together on its council, practical help came from the Rotary Club and support from other organisations. Committees changed; secretaries and other officers came and went; Sister Julia continued, pioneering responses to needs of all kinds. It was she who was the focal point of the enterprise. Above all, it was she who held the growing trust of teenagers as well as children, men as well as women. She, more than anyone, saw the transformation God was working in individual human lives.

Operation Friendship still exists, though slum-dwellers have been moved and squatter areas bulldozed by government order. Nursery schools and basic schools, adult education and literacy classes, medical clinics with half-a-dozen doctors, dental clinics and family planning groups are all to be found on Ebenezer premises from which the young deaconess first looked across her frightening parish. Scholarships to secondary schools and a trade training centre were made possible by Rotary interest. University students and overseas volunteers share in the work. The churches are more fully involved, their conservatism challenged by people they would once have preferred to forget.

Behind all the movement is the quiet figure of Sister Julia. Behind the deaconess who began it all is the direction and power of God.

In 1972 God gave a new direction to Sister Julia's life. She was appointed to Haiti, to share in meeting needs as acute as those in Western Kingston—to go on building new bridges of friendship and love.

VOODOO ISLAND

Marco Dépestre wakened his wife in the middle of the night. Had he been suffering from a vision or a nightmare? Plainly, as he came back to consciousness, it was no more than a dream. He had thought he was dead—and discovered that no one really cared. In this moment of humiliation he heard a voice. 'If you *were* dead—who would look after your wife and children?' The dream passed, with its horror, but the voice remained in his ears. That was why he wakened his wife. Marco had been trying to decide for many months whether or not he ought to offer himself as a candidate for the Methodist ministry. Now he knew the answer: God would care for his family.

In the small hours of the night he and his wife pledged themselves to the purposes of God.

It was no easy choice, for Marco had come to this moment by no ordinary road.

Haiti, indeed, is no ordinary land. Part of the second largest island in the Caribbean, it was the first all-negro republic, and from the days of the black Emperor Christoph it has known violence. The mixture of Catholic practice and popular superstition manifests itself in voodoo, a secret cult whose drums throb across the plains and mountains. The country's middle-class rulers were ousted by 'papa Doc' Duvalier, who became a dictator and reigned without further elections with the aid of a widely-dispersed secret service whose agents were the *tontons macouts*, the dark-spectacled 'bogey men' with revolvers and tommy-guns.

In the small town of St Marc, Dépestre *père* was a doctor with some literary skills, and young Marco was often sent to the printers with his pamphlets. He would stand and watch while they were set up. But the Dépestre family was well-off compared with the peasants who thronged the streets on market-days. Sometimes on donkeys, more often on their heads, they brought the small supplies of grain, yams or fruit they had managed to grow on their subsistence-level farms. Poverty and malnutrition were built-in disabilities of Haitian rural life, along with illiteracy, fear and negligible medical assistance. One of the obvious ways of helping the situation was for Marco to follow his father's profession. Instead of becoming a doctor, however, he chose to become an agronomist, serving in the government Department of Agriculture. Until his younger brother died, leaving Marco with thoughts of eternity which jostled with his professional concern for earthly betterment, he had never thought of becoming anything else.

Though a devout Roman Catholic, he read the Bible for the first time when he was loaned one by a friend. It led him to explore church after church until he was received into the Methodist Church on Easter Day. Twenty years earlier there had been discussions about withdrawing Methodist missionaries from Haiti. If nothing else did so, Marco Dépestre justified their decision to stay. In 1948 he came back to his own country as a minister, after theological training in Jamaica.

He was stationed in the little country town of Petit Goave, at the foot of the mountains.

The achievements of the years that followed are stupendous.

He quickly found that he must be more than a preacher of the gospel in the conventional setting of a local church. It was important that people should be able to study further what he said in the pulpit. This meant literature—books, pamphlets, hymns. But in a country where the official language is French the majority of the people spoke Creole, dismissed until then as a *patois* of the ignorant. Creole had no literature at all. Behind the bastardised French pronunciation and idioms Marco began to discover a grammar with African roots. He began literacy classes in Creole, and was decorated by the government with the Order of Honour and Merit for his work. Able to read—what? An Irish missionary produced a Creole hymn-book and translated the services of the church into that language. Then the American Bible Society asked Marco to translate the Gospels and the Acts into Creole, and soon they were circulating amongst the people.

Marco thought back to the days when his father had sent him to the printers. Printing was expensive. Why should not the Church do its own? He set up a printing press in a shed behind the manse. Within a few years he had been asked by the committee of the American devotional booklet, *The Upper Room*, to print the French edition there. From the yard behind the manse copies of *La Chambre Haute* went out to twenty-eight French-speaking countries.

Marco's circuit consisted of twenty-two preaching-places. Few of them had conventional buildings and in many cases worship was conducted in private houses. Regular ministerial visits and worship were difficult to arrange, for roads were few on the plain and non-existent in the mountains. He began training-classes for new church members, and they were trained, catechised and examined in character as well as knowledge, and received into the life of the church by the score, year by year. There were classes for preachers and Sunday-school teachers, who would trek down overnight to Petit Goave once a month. Sometimes a prayer meeting would go on all night before they returned with lessons for the next month.

But Marco could never forget that he was an agronomist—'one of the best agricultural teachers in Haiti,' a government official once described him, 'for he has the confidence of all the 80,000 people amongst whom he lives.' Men must be prepared for eternity, but they must live in the world—and they should have proper means of livelihood. So there was a pig scheme, and a scheme with day-old chicks. There was a great campaign to get rid of rats, which devastated the crops. There was a farming co-operative and, not far from Petit Goave, a rural training centre offering three-month courses in farming and Christian leadership to young men, who took full advantage of it. Off the coast Marco visited the appallingly poor island of La Gonave, almost without water, and began to initiate cisterns and a de-salinisation plant to turn sea-water into fresh water. All-purpose churches and schools were built in the mountain villages—three schools for three hundred pupils each. In all this relief- and aid-agencies, both Christian and secular, co-operated with the church on the spot. 'Food for work' programmes provided five miles of new road.

In 1963 Hurricane Flora tore through the island at 160 miles an hour. Six months later another did the same. Marco discovered a mountain community of thousands of people starving after they had passed, and began relief work. He followed the hurricane, as he followed every trail that led to human need.

But it might be said, indeed, that the wind blows wherever Marco goes—the wind of change, of hope, the fresh air of the Spirit of God. In a troubled and poverty-stricken land the ministry of Marco Dépestre has been a sign of the power of the Gospel to transform the whole life of man.

14
Ina Disengomoka

CONGO DOCTOR

'That girl could be Congo's first champion in the Olympics!'

Africa was leaping into the news. The darkness of the so-called 'Dark Continent' was being dispersed with every day that passed. New governments were gaining new respect. New leaders were emerging of high quality, and already some were proving in the eyes of the world that statesmanship was not confined to the white nations or to Asia. In this process world sport had its own place.

Ina Disengomoka, still a teenager, had won the 150 metres and the high jump in her age-group in the national championships of Belgium. Training for the Olympics was offered to her as a serious possibility.

But Ina had another goal—another 'first'—in mind.

Her mother, Matondo Elizabeth, had often told her the story of how her own father had been the first boy in his village to go to school—to the horror of the old men and women, who believed that 'marks on paper that could talk' were white men's magic which would destroy the black man's soul. She had told her, with more detail, her own story . . . how, at the age of twelve, she had been sent on a fifty-mile walk, balancing her few belongings on her head, to that same school at Ngombo Lutete.

'Your name,' said the schoolmaster-missionary, 'is Matondo—"Thanksgiving". I give thanks to God for your coming to this school—and I pray that others will thank God for you.'

Before she left school Matondo was helping in the mission's baby clinic, taking temperatures, working in the maternity ward, even delivering babies. She thought perhaps that this was where her work would lie, that she would be a nurse. Instead, she married a teacher, Émile Disengomoka, in 1939. First as a teacher, then a headmaster, and later a director of village schools, Émile needed all the help his wife could give him. As one child after another arrived, until there were eight altogether, the teenage dreams of nursing faded away.

But not, perhaps, completely away.

Ina's parents were immensely proud of their teenage daughter's triumphs in Belgium. In their secret dreams they had never imagined that one of their children would be surrounded with reporters the moment she stepped off an airplane at Kinshasa, that her photograph would appear in Belgian and Congolese papers, that an Olympics gold medal would be a possibility for one of their children.

They wondered what Ina would do; whether she would be prepared to undertake the years of hard training essential to athletic triumph. It would be a long road, with no guarantee of success at the end.

Ina chose a longer road still, and one which required yet more discipline.

First at school, working hard to gain the necessary examination successes, and then in Belgium, far from home, in college and university, Ina worked on courageously. Her father died before she even knew that he was ill. Olympics came and went, with no names from the Congo amongst the medallists. But, in June 1969, the names of Leon Nsumu and Ina Disengomoka, his wife, were read out in the crowded auditorium of the Brussels Medical School.

With their two small children they returned the following month to their own country, to serve their own people.

Ina Disengomoka brought to the Congo a greater distinction than any Olympic medal could have done. She had beaten a path which others will now follow. She is her country's first woman doctor.

UMBRELLA MAN

When Harry Eva was a small boy he was not allowed to walk on the left-hand side of the road on Sundays. Raspberries grew there and he might pick them. The trouble was not that he would be stealing but that he would be breaking the sabbath. It was a hard discipline after the dreary 'pleasure' of the Sunday afternoon—visiting the local cemetery and slowly spelling out the names on the gravestones. But Sunday was a weary business, anyway, with a two-and-a-half hour service in the morning and another almost as long in the evening.

Somehow, through all the rather narrow-minded religiosity of his parents, a vision of God broke through. God was indeed there, caring and faithful, and He was not the far-off and vindictive figure his mother and father painted.

Harry was to have deep and constant need of God in the years that followed.

When he was fourteen his parents died and, orphaned and homeless, Harry made his way from Vermont to Boston. Because he could not keep his clothes tidy on the five dollars a week he earned at his first job in a grocery store, he was sacked. With his wages taken for rent by his landlady Harry was turned on to the street with five cents in his pocket. He slept that night on a bench in a Boston park. Eight nights later, without work, and literally starving, he came back to the same familiar bench. No one noticed him; nobody cared. Why should they? There were too many ragged boys in well-to-do Boston.

Sitting on his park bench, eating his way through the one loaf of bread he was able to buy, Harry made a promise to God. If he should be preserved, should find work somehow, he would care for other homeless boys like himself.

Then on the ground by the bench, miraculously it seemed, he saw a cent in the snow. Trying to decide whether to buy a roll or a bun he determined to buy a paper instead and look at the 'situations vacant' column. The next day, although twenty-ninth in a queue of boys, he was given a job in a cafe, at six dollars a week.

Even though six dollars was hardly enough to pay for a room and something to eat, Harry started immediately to keep his resolve. Out of his weekly wages he put a few cents on one side. He did the same in his next job, and the next. But more than a few cents, or a few dollars, was needed. He went on working, and saving.

Harry Eva

At the end of nine years, Harry Eva had accumulated 400 dollars.

With his money is his pocket he set out to find a way of using it. From church to church, institution to institution, he went, offering his money. No one wanted Harry's money on the terms he laid down. It must be used to give food, clothing and shelter to stray boys, without any reference to their character or their creed. Need was the only qualification. In the end, shocked and disappointed, Harry faced facts.

If no one would take his money it must mean that God wanted him to do the job himself.

He moved from Boston to New York, and found a broken-down store. The landlord, to whom Harry told the whole story, not only gave him the use of the building for a small rent, but offered him a day-time job selling umbrellas. In the years that followed the umbrella-man became a familiar figure, working at his business in the day and scouting round the parks at night. He did not have to go far to find his first boy—a ragged, homeless child in Union Square—and before he reached the store that night he had collected five more. By the end of the week he had doubled the number.

It was clear that the 400 dollars, saved over nine years, might well be used up in almost as many weeks. The boys, all waifs and slum-children, were used to making money in simple if dishonest ways, and were disconcertingly cynical when Harry asked them to pray. 'If God wants me to do this,' he said, 'He will be even more interested in it than I am. He will supply our needs.' As the days went by it became clear that God was indeed 'interested'. Somehow, from somewhere, furniture, clothes, food and money came in.

There were bad times. With a debt of 260 dollars, and nothing to pay it with, he might well have given up hope. But a man who had defrauded his firm many years earlier and found it closed down when he wanted to repay the money, sent the 275 dollars to Harry instead. There was a time when there was no food at all, and a sixteen-pound ham was handed in from Mrs Theodore Roosevelt, widow of the ex-President of the United States. The stories could be multiplied almost endlessly.

In fifty years the Home for Homeless Boys, established by the 'umbrella man', gave shelter and a start in life to 50,000 boys. To the end of his life Harry Eva went on his nightly quest for more boys in need. To the end of his life the old, thin, rather shabby man proved that God always keeps His promises.

16
Bernard Fergusson

ONWARD, CHRISTIAN SOLDIER

In *Who's Who* the entry looks impressive. 'Brigadier Sir Bernard Fergusson, GCMG, GCVO, DSO, OBE . . . son of 7th baronet . . . Eton . . . Sandhurst . . .'. A long account of army service, followed by 'Governor-General, New Zealand'.

The man himself is impressive, too, but not by any means pretentious—tall, distinguished and assured, a Scottish aristocrat, now a life peer.

The record carries names and locations familiar to all who have lived through the Second World War and the period immediately preceding it: Palestine, Egypt, Suez, India, Burma. This is the record of a man of action. Yet the closing entries take us into another world. *Wavell; Portrait of a Soldier* and *Beyond the Chindwin* are very much more than military history. They are the work of a writer with a true feeling for words, and a perceptive judgment about his fellowmen. Poetry is there, too.

The soldier has had time for contemplation, not only of men and their works, but of God and His activity. This man is a committed Christian who has no reserve about declaring his faith.

For many people—an increasing number, indeed—the dilemma which they must resolve is posed most clearly by a man like Sir Bernard Fergusson. How can a soldier be a Christian?

He probably never intended to be anything other than a soldier. It ran in his blood. His father, also becoming Governor-General of New Zealand, was a general. The family's connexion was with the Black Watch, and young Bernard assumed that the historic regiment would be his own place, as indeed it was. He rose in time to be its colonel. Born in 1911, his name was down for Eton and, with a mind for history and English, he made his own contribution to its life before going on to Sandhurst. 'Very tough', he called it. Not even Eton had really reconciled him to Anglican worship and, with friends, he found his way to the Scottish kirk. It would not have occurred to him to try and evade what to most of his generation was a formality. He had been brought up to go to church. In his own phrase, he 'needed worship'.

There was little enough opportunity for it in many of the years that followed. He served in Palestine in the 1930's, spending most of his time on intelligence work and liaison with the Palestine police. When war came he served in the Middle East: then in India which he disliked because GHQ was a thousand miles or more from the war-fronts. Five times in his career he served with General Wavell, his undisguised hero, a man mostly silent but utterly uncorrupted by power. With the extraordinary Orde Wingate, an Old Testament warrior-prophet come to life, Fergusson shared the terrible rigours of the Chindit campaign in Burma, infiltrating the Japanese lines, cutting communications, running a guerilla war, leaving the wounded behind to die because they could not be carried. God seldom seemed a reality to most men involved in that campaign, where starvation was a more formidible enemy than the Japanese themselves, but 'more men—far more—showed how good they were, really good, than turned out badly'. So Fergusson, at any rate, discovered.

How could a man like Fergusson endure the anguish of seeing his soldiers die, their numbers diminishing day by day? His answer was clear. He believed that freedom was a gift of God to men, a gift to be prized above almost everything else. He once said, in answer to a question, that honesty, family morality and pride of craftsmanship were amongst the qualities he honoured most. Only a free society could make such things possible. To him, freedom was a gift which a Christian would die to preserve, and even if he must die soldiering through the desert and the jungle he would go on. Living or dying, God was there.

Looking back over his life, answering questions on a television programme, Fergusson could assert some things without reserve. The first was very evident. He shared the philosophy of George Borrow's gipsy; 'Life is very sweet, brother.' As he put it, he had had a life which was full of excitement, where one did not know what would happen next, yet there was one constant in all the changing circumstance. That constant factor was God. Not a remote and impersonal God, an object of worship on Sundays, forgotten during the week. 'I have never had any doubt. My belief has never failed in peace or war that God has a concern with us as individuals, and that when this life is over we shall continue as individuals in the presence of God.'

It is not surprising that, basing action on such belief, he could claim that his father's advice was unassailable. 'The best thing to do is always the right thing.'

17
Archibald Lang Fleming

THE FROZEN NORTH

'Any man can be a missionary . . . but not every man can build a ship!'

The Scottish sea-captain's son stood silent. All his life he had wanted to be a naval architect. School, university and night school had prepared him for his career, and he had been given rare opportunities in the great John Brown shipyards on the Clyde. Then two things came together—the memory of his sister talking about the Eskimo whom she had seen at a missionary meeting when Archibald was ten or eleven years old, and an advertisement in *The Life of Faith* for a young man courageous enough to face the hazards of the Arctic as a missionary. Now he stood before his employer, trying to hand in his notice.

It was in his autobiography that Fleming wrote these words. 'Only a man . . . with a glowing love of his Saviour and a pastoral heart could stand up to the hardship and loneliness of the Arctic.'

True, not every man could build a ship. But neither could every missionary be the sort of missionary that Fleming became.

In 1908 the young Scot, who had become an Episcopalian because there had not been a Presbyterian Sunday-school for him to attend, left for Canada. He was twenty-five years old and imagined himself training for the next few years for the priesthood in Toronto. Instead, the next year, his training was interrupted so that he might temporarily take over an empty mission-station in Baffin Land. With another missionary he set sail in the *Lorna Doone* for Lake Harbour, an isolated post at the extreme southern tip of Baffin Island.

Not even the stormy journey, in which baggage was flung about, the rigging torn and the snow-bound wastes of Labrador often out of sight, prepared him for what was to follow. Baffin Land was, as he said, 'on the edge of nothingness'—a desert of snow, ice and almost unceasing winter blizzards. The Eskimos, with only their brown mongoloid faces visible, spoke a language unlike anything he had ever imagined. Housing—apart from the mission house which they built and quickly deserted because there was no fuel to warm it—was no more than snow-blocks quickly cut and built into the soon-familiar igloos. It was in one of these that Fleming and his colleague Bilby spent the winter.

Based on Lake Harbour, with only an occasional summer visit from the trading ships, Fleming spent the next twenty-seven months isolated from almost everything he had hitherto thought of as civilization. Slowly he learned the Eskimo tongue, until at last he was able to preach in it. Month by month he sledged across the ice and into the blizzards behind the dog-teams, visiting Eskimo villages, sleeping in their huts filled with the odour of human beings, blubber-oil and seal-skin. With temperatures 80 degrees below zero and only melted snow water for washing even simple personal hygiene was a perpetual problem.

Slowly, too, he began to understand the people he had begun to love. Almost totally pagan, they were filled with the fear of evil spirits and dominated by the *angokok*, the sorcerer who was the most important man in every community. It was his joy, even on this first tour, to find people in most of the places he visited responding to the simple story of the Gospel. With retentive memories, through the lack of a written language, they quickly learned stories, hymns and even much of the prayer-book services. The joy in their faces as they listened to the Christmas story when they first heard it was something that Fleming never forgot.

Nor did he ever forget the terrible winter at Kinguckjuak. Living perforce with an Eskimo family in a crowded igloo he shared the growing privation as the spreading ice covered all the water channels and, for the first time, he faced not mere hunger but famine. To the end of his ministry this early sharing of disaster gave him a special unity with the Eskimo people and a special place in their hearts.

After a couple of years finishing his ordination studies he returned again to Baffin Land in 1913. Now Pudlo, a youth who had carefully questioned every statement of the Christian faith when he first heard it, was his constant companion and guide, and became the first Eskimo catechist. Change came, too, when the Hudson Bay Company opened a trading Post at Lake Harbour. By this time. however, Fleming was driving further afield behind his dog-team, penetrating to the north of Baffin Land where no white man had been before, and laying the foundations of the Church amongst the kindly, warm-hearted people who made their precarious living from hunting the arctic animals.

The work was more demanding than he dared admit, however, and in 1915, when he took furlough, he was declared medically unfit. Not for another five years did he return. 'The mind of Christ grows in the people,' he wrote. Much of this growth was due to his own work, but in the doing of it he ravaged his own health. Once he was almost drowned and his Eskimo helper was killed when their canoe overturned in a storm. That was only one hazard out of many and once again his missionary service was interrupted when he took leave. This time it was for six years at St.John's, New Brunswick.

When he went back it was as Archdeacon of the Arctic. His task was to travel throughout the northern part of four Arctic dioceses and he became as familiar with the work amongst the Indians as he had been with that amongst the Eskimo. The long reaches of the Mackenzie river took him to Aklavik, on the edge of the sea beyond the Arctic circle.

At last, in 1933, the Bishopric of the Arctic was established. It was a post no man could really fill but Fleming.

By rail, schooner, canoe, aeroplane and motorboat he travelled 14,000 miles in his first year as bishop. There were schools to be established thoughout the whole Hudson's Bay region; medical work to be done; a hospital to be built at Aklavik, which later burned down in the waterless winter when he was visiting it. Because the missionary society which supported him was in financial straits he had to raise money for all his new ventures himself. 'Archibald the Arctic'—which Lord Tweedsmuir (John Buchan) called 'the most romantic signature in the world'—became a familiar one on letters of appeal. On British television he made the first missionary appeal ever.

In a diocese of one and a quarter million square miles he was always on the move, speaking to his beloved Eskimo people in their own tongue and reaching the hearts of the Indians even when he did not know their language. For the inroads of 'civilisation'—the mines, the military camps and new lines of communication—he had little liking, though he knew they were inevitable, but he exercised his ministry amongst the white men with as much devotion as he had done in his pioneering days amongst the Eskimo.

When at last, in 1946, he had to retire because of ill-health, after almost fifty years of missionary service, he had made the sort of mark few men ever leave. He was one of the makers of the far North and will remain one of the great folk-heroes of Canada. With Moravians, Lutherans and men of other denominations than his own, he had taken the Gospel to those who had never heard it and established the Church. To the end he remained faithful, courageous and high-hearted.

Not every missionary can be such a missionary as Fleming.

THE NEVER NEVER LAND

Australians call the interior of their vast continent the 'outback' or the 'Never Never Land'. It was there that John Flynn made his name—and made it world-famous. But he did more than make a name, he changed the life, and saved the lives, of thousands of families throughout the remote areas of these sparsely-populated regions.

He founded what is now the Royal Flying Doctor Service of Australia.

But that was only part of his gift to the people of the outback. Before the Flying Doctor ever took to the air Flynn had begun the organisation on which it was first based—the Australian Inland Mission of the Presbyterian Church.

It began when he followed the Birdsville track for five hundred miles and came to Oodnadatta, a small desert township which, despite its size, was the main supply point for Central Australia at a time when the only transport was horse and wagon. It was set in the midst of hundreds of square miles of arid plains where the only life seemed to be the yellow flower of the mulga plant. The ironstone fragments of the plains, smoothed by sand and wind, gave rise to mirages of great stretches of water. Mirages they were, indeed. Flynn found that the average rainfall was only seven inches a year, in a land where the temperature for long weeks on end seldom dropped in the daytime below 120 degrees.

Born in 1880 in a mining town in the state of Victoria, Flynn served as a teacher for four years before he joined the Home Mission staff of the Presbyterian Church of Victoria. 'Home Missions' meant not so much working in the slums of the great cities as reaching out to the remoter townships which had sprung up, more particularly in the mining areas. At the beginning of the present century Australia, to most people who had never been there, was a country to which criminals had been transported and which had now become respectable, a country with only a few sizeable towns—Brisbane, Melbourne, Sydney, Perth—and the average man in Britain would have been hard put to it to think of any others. It was a land of wool and wheat, and the mining towns. To tell the truth, in so large a country, many Australian town-dwellers would not have known much more about their own land, either.

Of the desert which stretched endlessly behind the coastline they heard frightening tales of hardship and lost lives. Of the Northern Territory they knew nothing, except that the Aborigines lived there.

It was into some of the remote outposts that John Flynn was sent in 1912, the year after he had been ordained and stationed at Beltana, a mining town in the outback. His report stirred and shocked the Assembly of his Church, making it clear that 'something must be done'. This, however, is a dangerous doctrine to enunciate. The man who proclaims it is likely to find that it recoils on himself. So it was with John Flynn. The year he made his dramatic report on the hardships, the loneliness, indeed the godlessness he had found as he travelled the Birdsville track and others like it, the Australian Inland Mission was created and he himself was made its superintendent for two years.

He was to remain in charge of it for thirty-nine years.

The 'Inland', so far as the Mission was concerned, was not a concentrated tract of country but an immense area stretching from South Australia to the Northern Territory. The sporadic homesteads and wooden-frame townships needed the word of the Gospel, and this was proclaimed by ministers, many of them young, riding horseback, much as the 'circuit riders' of the Methodists had done in the pioneering days of the American prairies. But Flynn knew well enough that people needed this word confirmed in practical ways, and his preachers were initiated into at least a minimal amount of medical knowledge. Soon nursing services were set up by the Mission, always with two nurses ('who must be able to get on well together') to run clinics which might well be five hundred miles or more from the nearest town of any size. Welfare centres and clubs provided an alternative to the rough drinking saloons.

But it was evident that still more was needed. If there were real emergencies with which nurses, however skilled, could not deal, what then? If doctors were needed, how could they reach the outback?

How, indeed, could they *know* when and where they were needed?

By the 1920's two modern advances were beginning to affect the whole world. One was the increasing use of aircraft; the other was radio. Australia had been in the forefront of aerial pioneering, and Flynn was not long in seeing that here was a completely new means of serving the people of the outback. The other problem remained. Even if it were possible to broadcast to the 'Never Never Land' they could not, on their part, transmit their own needs. Would it be possible to devise a simple radio-set, cheap enough to instal widely, powerful enough to cover large distances over the desert country, and which would at the same time be a receiver and transmitter?

It was a young South Australian electrical engineer, Alfred Treager, who produced a light, compact pedal-radio, which was easy to operate and repair and generated its own electricity. This was the moment of breakthrough. The silence of the outback was truly broken. A new day of service and hope had come. It would clearly be possible not only to use the transmitter to call for help, but to use the receiver—despite its vulnerability to static and other limitations—so as to take instructions about treatment from doctors far away.

In 1928 Flynn set up the first radio base at Cloncurry, Queensland, and began to supervise the installation of the Treager pedal-receivers throughout the region. A doctor was engaged, and an aircraft chartered from Queensland and Northern Territory Aerial Services—now the gigantic QANTAS line. In May of that year Arthur Affleck, a twenty-five-year-old QANTAS pilot, made an entry in his logbook. '15.5.28 . . . Commencement Aerial Medical Services'. Dr St. Vincent was called to a patient as soon as the plane touched down in Cloncurry. It was the first service rendered by the Flying Doctor, and the call was dealt with before the speeches of congratulation could begin.

From that day the vision of John Flynn became reality. In his own words 'the inland was covered by a mantle of safety'. For him, the practical and the spiritual were both aspects of the caring grace of God.

Today the outreach of the Service is spectacular. In 1970 there were 3,451 flights, covering more than a million and a half miles; 3,451 patients transported; 73,910 consultations, over 20,000 of them by radio. Homes in the RFDS area have a standard medicine chest, with anatomical charts and a numbered index of contents. Radio diagnosis is based on the patient's symptoms or needs, and an actual visit is by no means always essential.

John Flynn, who died in 1951, is buried near Alice Springs, His grave is marked by a 'devil's marble', a granite monolith. At the Centralian Crossroads the Governor-General unveiled a cairn in his memory. The Presbyterian Church at Alice Springs has a museum which includes the first radio transceiver ever used.

But the real memorial to John Flynn, who pioneered the Inland Mission of his own Presbyterian Church, is in changed lives and healed bodies throughout the land that few people knew and fewer cared about.

19
Evangeline French

ANY ONE OF THREE

The 'three' were Evangeline French, her sister Francesca, and their life-long colleague, Mildred Cable. To write about any one of them is, inevitably, to write about all three. They worked and wandered together, they lived together in China and after they left it. They spoke together on the same platforms, especially in the service of the Bible Society. They shared the same faith and the same attitude to life. Yet, because their temperaments were so different, not only was it possible for them to work in harmony but to contribute infinitely more than any single one of them could have achieved with other colleagues.

Eva was the first of them to go to China. The year was 1893. More than a world away in time as well as distance, her work spanned what now seems a remote period of China's history and the days when Japan invaded from the East and Russian forces were infiltrating from the north. Not until the 1960's, when she was over ninety, did she die.

Born in North Africa and growing up in Geneva, the French sisters moved to England before Queen Victoria's diamond jubilee. In Portsmouth Eva, always rebellious, reacted bitterly against the poverty of the slums and the conservative respectability of the churches which acted as though the squalid hovels did not exist. She once told her sister that, if she could, she would take the world's misery on her own shoulders and leap into the sea. Francesca reminded her that this very thing had been done by Jesus Himself, on the cross. Within a week or so Eva had found a new peace, and a new purpose in life.

Going to China with the China Inland Mission she took three weeks to reach Shansi by cart along the interminable roads, and for the next seven years served the villagers of the district. In Chinese dress, with a growing knowledge of Chinese thought, custom and language, she became one of China's own millions. With them she endured the horrors of the Boxer Rising in 1900, often in danger of death and escaping by the narrowest of margins time after time as she made her way to the coast. It was a horror-story which ended a whole period of Chinese history. Eva left for her first furlough as scores of missionaries and thousands of Chinese Christians were being killed for their faith.

When she returned to China Mildred Cable went with her, and her sister Francesca joined them not long afterwards.

Eva spent another twenty years in Shansi—almost thirty in village work altogether. The urgent need was for the building up of the Church, for the training of its own leadership and especially for the emergence of responsible Christian women and girls. In the town of Hwochow they had their base. There Mildred and Francesca began a school for girls which was eventually to include a teacher-training establishment. From Hwochow Eva went out into the surrounding countryside, taking the gospel to the villages. Another revolution came and went. The old China ended as the Republic took the place of the Emperor, and Sun Yat Sen became President. There was a new and guaranteed place for many of those Christian women who had passed through Hwochow.

'The Three', as they called themselves, had always seen this Shansi work as an episode in their ministry rather than the whole of it. Hwochow was a base, not the end of the trail. Their aim was to encourage the emergence of an independent Chinese Church, neither a pale copy of the Western Church nor something dependent on it for leadership, money or direction. When they planned to go farther inland, and the Shansi congregation pleaded with them to stay, the Chinese Christians said: 'If you stay we will do whatever you tell us!' The promise confirmed their fears and their assurance that it was God's will they should move on. To stay was to provoke the sort of future for the Church they most wished to avoid.

In 1923, in the words of the title of their own book, they passed *Through Jade Gate and Central Asia*.

For the next fifteen years they were to be pioneers in the Gobi Desert.

The Gobi is the largest desert in the world, its cities set in large oases. These towns were the meeting-grounds of Chinese, Tibetans, Turkis, and Mongols. Their population was Muslim, Buddhist, animists, ancestor worshippers and devil-worshippers. Christians were a negligible minority in numbers and in many places did not exist at all. As they trekked slowly along the Old Silk Road, on the first part of their journey, they came every week or so upon Christian mission stations. Beyond Kanchow there were none. They were indeed pioneers.

Now Mildred's long period of school-teaching was over—though she was to remain an educationist to the end of her life. All three were missionaries in the traditional sense of the word. Only a few Chinese fellow-workers had gone with them and they had to build the Church in very much the same sense that it was built in the time of the Apostles. They were as certain of the presence, the power and the direction of God as the New Testament pioneers themselves.

The first priority was to work out a method of evangelism suitable to this sparsely-populated desert region where the Christian gospel and women preachers were equally extraordinary. Two elements in this new strategy were quickly apparent. They must talk to people, and give them something to read which would last when the itinerant encounter was over. Naturally, they had to move widely about the district for had they stayed in one place they would have met only a few people. So they became travelling evangelists. They bought a cart and collected teams of mules and with them they travelled the desert. Mildred Cable's description of their activity was 'gossipping the gospel', though it was always a purposeful sort of gossip. Lamas in the lamaseries, Buddhist priests in monasteries, traders with their camel caravans, soldiers in temporary garrisons, bandits and brigands on their ruthless way, women at the markets—these were their gossip-partners. If they could read the listeners often asked for a book. So the Bible Society came into its own. In the multitude of languages of Central Asia they provided Gospels, Testaments and Bibles which found their way into remote towns to which European women would not penetrate for half a century. Thus the gospel made its way into Tibetan villages, Mongol tents and Muslim homes.

Books like *Something Happened, A Desert Journey* and especially *The Gobi Desert* showed the intellectual quality of the three women. Recognition by learned societies paid tribute to their observation as well as their courage.

In 1936 they were forced to leave. The Japanese had begun waging undeclared war on the Chinese people and the Gobi was being infiltrated by Russian advance-parties. All missionaries were expelled.

In Britain they wrote and spoke continuously. The war found them in the West Country and then in London, giving service to the Bible Society. They undertook a long speaking tour to India, Australia, New Zealand and the Pacific—and another in 1949 to South America. Their books were best-sellers. Few names were better known in church circles.

In the Gobi Desert even their Chinese names may have been forgotten, though their legend will live on in places they never saw. This would matter little to any of the three. What did matter was that the gospel had been preached. The word, widely scattered, must bear fruit even in the parched and arid lands of Central Asia.

HE HAS NO MAGIC

'We need a man to call America back to God'.

The words were burned on the young student's heart at the Florida Bible Institute. He did not see himself as *the* man to do this, though probably more than any evangelical crusader of his generation he has done just that, but he was deeply certain that it was his mission to share in the task. Unlike some famous names in the world of 'mission' he did not see himself as a born preacher, or even a great one, but he could say from the beginning, after his conversion, that he had a 'passion for souls'.

Born in North Carolina in 1918, he would not be mistaken for anything other than a Southerner. It is not from these states, in the main, that the political rebels or theological radicals have come. Certainly there were few of them in the Southern Baptist Convention into which Billy was ordained in 1939. But those of his critics who deny that he had any concern with social ethics or poverty and race problems miss the point of his ministry. To Billy Graham the cause of all these ills lies in the sinfulness of the human heart. He will not denounce or criticise those who are committed to social action, and he has recently become active in this field himself, but he will not let it be said that this is the whole of the Gospel, or even its main concern. He believes, and preaches, that nothing will really change men's hearts, or an evil social system, but the grace of Jesus Christ. It is this which he is called to proclaim, in many places and in a variety of ways. It is this, he believes, which the Bible itself asserts.

To Billy, the Bible—all of it—is the Word of God. It seems always to be in his hand.

He quickly found there were to be other avenues than the normal pastorate open to him. Going to Wheaton College, near Chicago, to further his education by an anthropology course before entering a theological college, he was asked to undertake a part-time pastorate at the United Gospel Tabernacle. Here he had students and professors in the congregation. It was a useful apprenticeship, but he had a conviction that he ought to enter the Army as a chaplain. Instead, his professors persuaded him to take another pastorate, at Western Springs. A neighbouring Baptist pastor, Torrey Johnson, offered him the opportunity of taking over *Songs in the Night*, three-quarters of an hour of music and preaching every Sunday on one of Chicago's most powerful radio stations. Overwhelmed, Billy sought out a young Canadian singer and programme-manager of the American Broadcasting Corporation, Beverly Shea. It was Shea, not Billy Graham, who pulled in the audience in the beginning, but Billy very quickly established himself as a compelling broadcaster.

Torrey Johnson, again, offered him a second opportunity which helped to establish the pattern of his future ministry. A young businessman, seeing the hundreds of servicemen who thronged Chicago, organised a 'Youth for Christ' Rally. Johnson took up the idea, booked Chicago's three thousand-seat Orchestra Hall for twenty-one Saturday nights—and chose Billy for the opening rally. There were songs, music, community singing, scripture readings—and then the sermon. Over forty young people came forward in commitment that first night.

'Youth for Christ' began to spread throughout America with its motto: 'Geared to the Times, Anchored to the Rock'. All over the States Billy proved a powerful draw. In 1946 the team took a whirlwind three-week tour through England, Scotland and Ireland to launch Youth for Christ in Europe.

Back in the States Billy Passed through a turmoil of soul. Close friends began to question the validity of the Scriptures and Billy was torn one way and the other. In the end, as he has said, he went out into the moonlight, put his Bible on a tree-stump, knelt down and prayed. 'Oh God, I cannot prove certain things . . . I cannot answer the questions some people are asking . . . but I accept this Book by faith as the Word of God'.

It is an assertion on which he has never turned his back.

The years that followed proved, for Billy, the rightness of his decision. There was, first, a wonderful campaign in Los Angeles, with men brought to Christ who were to prove of great significance in the Graham campaigns of the future. This campaign, scheduled to last three weeks, was through the popular demand of the people extended to eight weeks. Following Los Angeles Billy was scheduled to conduct a campaign in Boston in 1950. It was feared that his overwhelming success in Los Angeles would be overshadowed by failure in Boston. Because of the predominance of Roman Catholics, the pride, reservedness, and self confidence of the people his acceptance was not expected. The campaign was to be held in the Park Street Congregational Church. However, due to the crowds who overflowed the church on the first two nights it became apparent that another larger area must be found. First it was moved to Mechanics Hall, then to the Opera House, back to the Mechanics Hall and finally ended in the Boston Garden. The Boston campaign was indeed a success.

During this campaign and in the following Columbia campaign the

Graham "team" began to be built. A member of considerable significance was Ruth Graham, Billy's wife, who had a valuable sense of humour which never permitted her husband to get over-elated or, for that matter, unduly depressed.

1950 was a year of immense importance, for through the death of one of the premier religious broadcasters a nationwide programme became available. Yet to Billy and his team it seemed practically and financially impossible. It would be a weekly broadcast, making immense demands on time, and it would cost an initial $25,000 to take up the option. Billy decided to make the financial test the immediate one. At a campaign meeting in Portland, Oregon, he told the audience that he needed the money, and why. Then he stood with an empty shoebox. Before he went to bed he had precisely $25,000.

The *Hour of Decision* programme was born, and in its first five weeks reached the highest-ever audience-rating for a religious programme. Within five years it was being broadcast by more than eight hundred and fifty stations all over the world.

The following year Billy's first film, *Mr Texas*, a 'Christian Western', was released and two years later his first book, *Peace with God*, leapt into the best-seller bracket. He had gained much in confidence, was able to make the most of every new opportunity and had become a world figure. But his confidence was never in himself or in his team. It remained firmly fixed in God. However much he suffered from nerves or distrusted his own decisions, as he often did, prayer remained the dominant activity of his life, for only through it could trust in God be made effective.

Amongst the campaigns of the 50's and 60's—and they took him not only to Europe, but to Africa, Asia and the Pacific—the most memorable was the New York Crusade held in Madison Square Garden in 1956. Graham's invitation and acceptance to come to New York brought the most violent opposition he had yet received. However, despite the opposition, the Crusade broke all records in attendance, in decisions, and in impact on the city. The Crusade lasted sixteen weeks and ended with a rally in Times Square which was the largest gathering Graham has ever addressed. When the Crusade was over the executive secretary of the Protestant Council of New York wrote to Billy Graham and told him he felt that four great accomplishments had been made: persons had been won to Christ, the city had become God-conscious, the churches had been strengthened and the city had become conscious of moral, spiritual, and social responsibilities.

Probably the problem which most distresses Billy Graham throughout his campaigns is the matter of follow-up.

For a century the evangelical campaign has been familiar, with its choirs and soloists, its build-up of speakers and its great name, its emotional, reiterated appeal and its trickle or torrent of 'converts' coming forward. Not least familiar has been the almost immediate loss of many who came forward. The likelihood of such 'falling away' is intensified when crowds are immense, and enquirers are often far from home and likely to be without religious affiliations.

Accepting these contemporary disabilities and the lessons from the past Billy Graham decided, from the beginning of his public ministry, to work in the closest possible cooperation with the churches. Out of this concern the follow-up plan was developed. Each person who comes forward is met by a counselor on a one-to-one basis and is told to do five things: read the Bible, pray, witness, live a consistent life for Christ at home and in business, and most important go to church. After the counselor, who has been trained beforehand, has finished counseling and instructing, he or she asks the person to fill out a decision card which enables the information to go immediately to the appropriate local minister. This process was perfected during the campaigns in 1953 and has been used in all of his campaigns since.

The significant difference, then, between the Graham Crusade technique and most of his predecessors and contemporaries, is an honest and fervent desire to work closely with any and all the churches, both before and during a campaign. He believed that a decision was no more than the word implied. It was a beginning. Growth lay in the local fellowship of Christian people.

For Billy himself, however, the tragedy was that his campaign divided rather than united churches. Mistrusting his fundamentalist theology, or attacking him for concentrating on personal decision for Christ rather than on social evils, political issues or world situations, some radical Christian writers and speakers saw his work as introspective and isolationist. Billy saw such men, for many of whom he had personal respect, as dealing with symptoms instead of the disease itself. Evil in society is the result of sin in the human heart; Billy Graham has no doubt about that. Nor has he any doubt that only the power of God can conquer sin and change society. He has seen it happen again and again, in every part of the world.

THE MIDDLE OF HELL

'You can't play in the dirt all day and not get filthy.'

That was the confirmed attitude of many good, honest and respectable Baptists when they heard what was happening in Bourbon Street, New Orleans. They were joined in their high-minded condemnation by Methodists, Episcopalians, Catholics. The cynical comments of non-churchgoers were even more strident.

Bob Harrington, Baptist minister with red socks, red pocket-handkerchief, red tie and a red-covered Bible, proved them wrong. So have hundreds of other tough, dedicated Christian men and women all over the world. Bob Harrington dedicated his life to getting down in the dirt. He has not managed to sweep it away. It is still there. But his life is spent in trying to lift men and women, not least young women, out of it.

Born in a tiny town, Sweet Water, Alabama, in 1927, he was fortunate to have a prosperous home in the midst of an area of grinding poverty. Perhaps life was too easy. He was certainly spoiled—an arrogant boy who admired only the tough and the successful. In any game he had to be the leader—though in football or anything else he was prepared to work hard for success. Indeed, because he worked so much harder than most of his competitors, success seemed to drop into his hands. He played harder, too, and as a result, after an abortive period at a military training school and then at the Great Lakes Naval Training Station, which ended when the Japanese surrendered and the war was over, he got a football scholarship to the University of Alabama.

Soon he was married to a childhood sweetheart, a Baptist girl called Joyce Compton. All too soon she found that he was hard-drinking, unprincipled and unfaithful. From an ambition to be a doctor he turned to photography and then, because money did not come quickly enough, to insurance. It was a way of life in which he excelled—selling insurance, selling hope, selling himself. His best business was done in the honky-tonks, the bars, the dives where businessmen forgot their wives and their sober homes. Because it was done at night he saw less and less of his wife and family. That was a loss he did not worry about. By the time he was thirty, he had joined the 'Million Dollar Club'—the exclusive ring of those who had sold a million dollars' worth of insurance.

Brash, noisy, highly-charged, successful—but not happy—Bob

Harrington was hollow inside, and frightened in case someone found out.

It was in April 1958, that he astonished his mother and father by going to a revival meeting at the Baptist church in Sweet Water. That night he was converted—stopped dead in his tracks by God and turned completely about.

Almost at once he began to sell his religious faith with even more energy than he had sold insurance. He witnessed and prayed in churches, in Rotary clubs, with the police who stopped him for speeding, with the psychiatrist to whom his wife sent him for help and treatment. Not only witnessed to them about his new-found faith, but won them, too. Then almost at once, it was no longer insurance-selling, but evangelism full-time. In revival-meetings, in cafeterias and the open-air, in a van covered with texts and his own name—'Bob Harrington, Evangelist'. In many people the extrovert, vivid, often insensitive, enthusiasm would have seemed only exhibitionism, doomed to die away as the days passed. With Harrington the conviction grew that this was what he had been born for—'born again' for, he would have said.

With no job and no money the future for his family seemed uncertain. Then, accepted as a student at the New Orleans Theological Seminary, he was also appointed as an assistant to Dr Grey, minister of the First Baptist Church. Highly charged, almost super-charged with energy and enthusiasm, and with an evangelical 'passion for souls', he was all over the old queen-city of the Mississippi—in a dozen different directions every day.

The first certainty of direction came when Dr Grey sent him into the French Quarter—the traditional, highly-sensationalised vice-quarter of the city—to try and win back a businessman who had deserted his wife to go and live with a prostitute. Failing in the task—and the discipline of failure was as frequent as the glow of success—he suddenly saw Bourbon Street for what it was. 'The middle of hell', Billy Graham called it.

On the face of it Bourbon Street was filled with bars, strip-clubs, drunks, drug-addicts, sensation-seeking tourists—vice of every kind, degradation from end to end. Below the surface, it was composed of men and women, youths and girls seeking escape and almost entirely without happiness or hope. Equally clearly, he saw that Bourbon was where God wanted him to be.

For ten years he has been 'the chaplain of Bourbon Street', as the mayor of New Orleans named him on a television programme. He is the only man whose regular Sunday pulpit is the stage of a strip-club, and one of the few men who can move with freedom and without embarrassment in and out of the dressing-rooms of strippers and the bawdy cellars of the night-clubs. A hundred thousand dollars are spent in a night in this street. Bob Harrington may not alter it, but he changes people's lives, almost every day and night. He brings to safety the would-be suicide on a window-ledge high above the crowd. He sends a man home to his wife; gives a stripper the courage to go back and face her parents, or to start a worthwhile job far away from New Orleans; brings a drug-addict from addiction and despair to freedom and hope.

Now he travels a hundred thousand miles a year, runs a telephone service for those in despair, and is known far outside the United States.

But Bourbon Street is really his home.

Bourbon Street is where the action is.

Bourbon Street is where God is.

UNDER THE SKIN

Trevor Huddleston belongs to that class of British society which, over the last century, has shown an astonishing genius for penetrating the barriers that separate one social group from another. Deriving from an aristocratic family, he has exercised compassion without condescension, and followed his Lord in love for those whom the privileged despise. Like the Old Testament prophet, his demand has been that justice should roll like a mighty stream. That the dams of prejudice and self-interest have held back justice has raised in him a vehement anger and opened yet deeper springs of compassion within him.

Nought For Your Comfort, the soul-searing account of his years in Sophiatown, a world best-seller, perhaps opened more eyes and made more enemies than most books of its decade.

It is probably true that to Huddleston the colour of a man's skin matters less than anything else about him. Spare of figure, ascetic of countenance, Huddleston arrived in South Africa in 1943, at the age of twenty-nine. He had been sent as priest-in-charge of the Sophiatown and Orlando Anglican Mission, a normal missionary posting by a Society which expected its members to be more sensitive than most missionaries. Huddleston, not so much choosing the Church as a vocation as being chosen by God for it, had joined the Community of the Resurrection, whose mother-house is at Mirfield in Yorkshire. A monastic Order within the Church of England, its members are vowed to poverty, chastity and obedience. The Community expects of its members a particular awareness of social needs and ills, and a readiness to respond to them.

Sophiatown could hardly have made these needs and ills more blatantly plain. It was the setting which Alan Paton, the South African novelist, had chosen for *Cry, the Beloved Country*. The contrast with white Johannesburg, in whose homes and industries many of its people worked, struck Huddleston immediately as appalling. Instead of the spacious and pleasant homes and gardens of the white city, the black people lived in restrictive poverty. Much, though by no means all, of Sophiatown was squalid lines of small hutments in which human dignity was desperately hard to maintain. At the same time, it included one of the very few areas in South Africa where black people were able to own the land on which their homes were built. In this part of the township neat red-roofed homes were tidy and their owners proud of their achievements. Huddleston soon discovered that the existence of these small, dignified homes was more of an affront to the whites than the slums they condemned so violently. Such dignity and self-respect were a denial of their theory that Africans were less human than whites.

Because he identified himself completely with his black parishioners, his church was crowded. In all he said it was clear that he thought of his congregation only as 'people', and that he understood the desperate struggle they had to maintain their integrity.

The most constant humiliation of *apartheid* was the pass-laws. To go anywhere, to live anywhere, the African must always be able to produce his 'pass', a piece of paper establishing his identity, his home area and so on. Without it an African is subject to fine or imprisonment. Of the 75,000 Africans jailed in Johannesburg two-thirds were pass-law offenders. The mere statement of a policeman was sufficient to obtain conviction. Huddleston devoted much of his time to helping those who were in trouble in this way. He would pay their fines to keep them out of prison and if possible he would try to intervene on their behalf. When Jonas, one of his schoolboys, was arrested as a vagrant, Huddleston was sure he was actually carrying his pass. He found Jonas beaten up in jail—and the boy's pass, torn up, in the waste-paper basket of the police-station.

Activities like this did nothing to endear the young priest to the authorities.

If to be without a pass was a crime which carried imprisonment, why not commit crimes that amount to something? This was a growing feeling amongst Africans, and the Johannesburg crime-rate rose alarmingly. In particular the *tsotsis*, teenage ruffians who hunted in gangs and engaged in violent robberies, rape and stabbings, terrorised black even more than white areas. Convinced that their behaviour was partly the result of a complete lack of recreational facilities, Huddleston began a club for them. Some he brought in as servers in his church. His own rooms were open to all who came.

When his Community offered seven acres of its land to the city council for an African recreational and community centre the project was turned down. In the *Rand Daily Mail* Huddleston pointed out that there were twelve public and three thousand private swimming pools for whites, and none for Africans. He appealed for funds to build a pool in Orlando. It took three years to raise the money, but when the pool was opened six hundred young Africans jumped in. Because of his practical concern, delinquency began to drop sharply.

Finding a boy longing for a trumpet 'to play like Louis Armstrong' Huddleston found him one. Before long he had established what became known as 'Huddleston's Jazz Band'. But he also opened wider doors in music, persuading top-rank African and visiting white artistes to play for his people. Yehudi Menuhin was one of them.

European children were given a free school meal each day; African children had none. Under his pressure, and that of other people who began to share something of his concern, a feeding scheme was extended to African schools—at a cost of twopence per day compared with sixpence spent on European children. But at least the barrier of indifference was broken.

Then, in 1954, the Malan government acted. African-owned houses in the neat, tree-lined streets of Sophiatown, houses proudly owned by those who lived in them, could be tolerated no longer. Africans were not fit to own anything at all. On 10th February, 1955, two thousand police moved into Sophiatown. The Western Areas Resettlement Act condemned Sophiatown and it was razed to the ground—not, of course, because Africans owned their own homes but because so much of the area was a shanty-town, made so by the restrictions and inhuman activities of white governments.

Nothing in his whole twelve years' residence affected Huddleston as did this act of brutal inhumanity. He wept openly as his people were dispersed to 'more suitable' areas.

'The Christian,' he wrote, 'if he is true to his calling, is always an agitator.' In the face of irrevocable opposition it was clear that Huddleston would be able to do little more for the people he loved. In 1956 his Community recalled him to Britain to train 'novices' for the Order. In his empty church, St Peter's, he sat and wrote the book which was to shock the world.

It was his last word from Johannesburg. But in Mirfield, and then back in Africa as Bishop of Masasi, and back once more in Britain as Bishop of Stepney, it proved to be far from his last word.

23
Annie James

BEAUTIFUL PEACE

She was not beautiful—just a plain, New Zealand country-girl from Otago, not more than five feet tall. Peace was the one thing she never really knew for at least half her service in China. Nevertheless they called her *Tse Koo*—in the Cantonese dialect it means 'Beautiful Peace'.

The name was well-chosen. Harassed by circumstance, war and banditry, broken by Communist interrogation, always with far more demands made on her than she could possibly meet, Annie James radiated the beauty of Jesus, and carried with her a sense of calm even when she was most under pressure.

'You can serve God by hoeing turnips on the farm' was the response made to her first offer to serve overseas. Soon afterwards a more percipient minister saw the qualities beneath the sun-roughened face and country-school accent of the teenager in his Dunedin congregation of St Andrews. Annie James, with the support of her Bible-class to see her through training-school, became 'St Andrew's Third Missionary' and left in 1912 to serve under the Presbyterian Missionary Society in Canton. Within two years she was back in New Zealand, invalided home.

Two years later she returned to China.

For the previous five years there had been revolution. Bandits and bullets were commonplace when Annie James was posted to Kong Chuen Hospital, at the beginning of her service, to nurse in the maternity block. Children were always to have a special place in her life—though it was a baby that finally put her in the Communist's power. For fifteen years she worked happily at Kong Chuen and then, after furlough in 1930, she was sent to take charge of an ancillary hospital at Kaai Hau, some fifty miles away. For seven more years she worked at the 'normal' routine tasks of the 'Hospital of Universal Love', dealing with some two thousand cases a year.

Then, on 7th July, 1937, the Japanese invaded China. Kaai Hau was on the main route from Hankow to Canton and, although in her remote village Annie took little notice of international affairs, it was not long before it was in the battle zone. She held on as long as she could, with Japanese soldiers and Chinese freebooters driving the hospital staff into hiding and robbing the hospital of food, medicines and blankets. At last not even her courage could stand the strain, and commonsense forced her to move into the mountains.

'The Hospital of Universal Love' became a mobile hospital, its whereabouts undisclosed to the Japanese but, somehow, always known to the peasants of the hills and valleys who sought it out wherever it went. Drugs were smuggled through the enemy lines, supplied by the Red Cross or by other hospitals. Once Annie herself made a perilous journey through occupied territory and then by air to Hong Kong to replenish her stocks. So, for seven years, life went on. She refused to obey the consul's call to leave. She saved the lives of children and adults, ministered under the most primitive conditions in bombed buildings and peasant huts, prayed courage into her nurses and made the presence of Christ real wherever she went.

By 1945 the war was over. The concentration camps were emptied. The bombing stopped. The 'Hospital of Universal Love' moved back to its shattered quarters at Kaai Hua.

Almost immediately there were new uncertainties. Mao Tse Tung, who had been plotting to unseat the Nationalist government when the Japanese should be driven out, came into the open. The seven years of war were succeeded by the Communist revolution. By 1950 Kaai Hua was under the rule of the Communists. Terror was let loose on the landlords, the intellectuals, the shopkeepers, the Christians.

The hospital, where the nurses shuddered as spies and informers openly walked into wards, private rooms and chapel, continued as best it could. A general's baby was brought into the children's ward, desperately ill. It died the night it was brought in.

Annie James was arrested, accused of killing it.

The charge was only an excuse. The real crime was that Tse Koo was a foreigner, and a Christian—an enemy of atheistic Communism.

She was questioned, starved, humiliated, and interrogated again and again. The rattle of the firing-squad sounded just outside the window of her cell, and the shouts of the crowds gathered to denounce one after another of their old leaders reverberated through the tiny room. She waited for the inevitable day when she too would be taken to the village square and the whole population, under dire penalties if they did not attend and shout as they were bidden, would turn out to yell their accusations.

The day came, at last. To her amazement, Annie James was led out into an empty town-square. No one in the whole town could be forced into the square to cry against her. For once, the will of the people prevailed. Not even fear of the Communist overlords could drive them to denounce one who had served them with such devotion.

Tse Koo, emaciated and ravaged with suffering, but triumphant in faith, was set free.

Two years later, after recuperating in New Zealand, she returned to Hong Kong, as near as she could get to the China she loved.

Today it is likely that no Christian congregations have been meeting regularly for worship in any part of Communist China for years. Was the service of Tse Koo, then, a waste of effort and a loss of all she strove for? In human terms what she worked and lived for has been swept away. But the end cannot be judged by human standards. Out of her labours came a nurse here and there, serving with dedication in Hong Kong or beyond China, a doctor and a surgeon offering skill with Christian compassion outside China's borders. For the rest, no one can say where faith burns because of Tse Koo's own faithfulness.

SAVE THE CHILDREN!

In 1969 the Save the Children Fund celebrated its golden jubilee. When it was founded it was intended to last for perhaps six weeks. Fifty years after its foundation it was operating in twenty-eight countries. It had over a thousand field workers—doctors, administrators, nurses, welfare workers, all fully trained and highly qualified. It had been involved in every major disaster area, every refugee problem, every war-torn country of the modern world. Its operations were costing over £5,000 a day. The problems it was organised to deal with had increased rather than diminished. Its future seems inevitable as long as there are children in the world who need care and help.

It began with a slim, poetry-loving, red-haired, gracious gentlewoman from a landed family in Shropshire—Eglantine Jebb.

One of six children, she was always the leader—the story-teller and the organiser of war-games. Born in 1876, she missed the first generation of women pioneers to break into the great universities, and studied history at Oxford, at Lady Margaret Hall. With a passion for books rather than people she began quickly to respond to the needs of children. Deliberately choosing to work amongst the unprivileged, she attended a teacher training college in east London and then taught for a year in a rural school in the little town of Marlborough. Then her health gave way.

She went to Cambridge to live with her widowed mother but instead of turning back to a leisured life she began seriously to investigate poverty. A convinced Christian—an Anglican by birth and choice—she did not believe that deprivation, hunger, dirt or disease amongst children could be tolerable to God, or to those who loved and served Him. Study gave place to action. The Balkan wars broke out in 1912. Where newspaper readers casually read accounts of the sufferings of soldiers and peasants, Eglantine Jebb vividly imagined the plight of the children. In 1913 she left home to work with the Macedonian Relief Fund. It was her first sight of the hungry, destitute, hopeless child-refugees to whom her life was to be given.

Before she had time to plan greater help for the Balkans the whole of Europe was plunged into war. The horror had expanded into countries she knew and loved—and behind the marching armies and the devastation of the shells she saw another army of starving, dying children. This was not the product of her vivid Celtic imagination. It was real and terrible truth, based on the facts her sister, Mrs Buxton, was collecting and publishing. By the end of the war, in 1918, it was conservatively estimated that there were thirteen million children in desperate need. In Eastern Europe four million were starving; Vienna, in particular, a city dear to cultured English folk, was little more than a death camp.

The two sisters decided to set up a society called the 'Fight the Famine Council'. Speaking all over the country, writing in the newspapers, they urged the government to act. Very quickly they saw that this was not enough. The aim must be sharpened in a way that would gain public support.

'We must begin a "Save the Children Fund",' declared Eglantine, 'and collect a thousand pounds for the starving children of Vienna.' That was in April, 1919. The first contribution was a half-crown from her own housekeeper. After a crowded meeting in the Albert Hall, contributions began to flow in. In a condemned house in Golden Square, London, with an ex-army table which is still in use, the two sisters began work. Quickly it was evident that Vienna was only a beginning. As letters and reports poured in, the magnitude of their task began to emerge.

Eglantine Jebb turned to the churches for support, and found it in considerable measure. She was received by the aged Pope Benedict XV, who issued a Papal Encyclical about the Fund—the first non-Catholic fund ever to be so commended. A service at St Martin-in-the-Fields was attended by Anglicans and Free Churchmen. The Orthodox Church pledged its support. Magazines, newspaper articles and films began to make real the task which faced post-war Europe. Austria was only the first of a dozen countries to receive help. One hundred and twenty million meals were served to the children of the Volga Valley in the terrible Russian famine, when they were eating straw and clay to assuage their hunger. By the time war broke out again between Turkey and Greece, the Fund had already spent a million pounds.

To Eglantine Jebb relief was not enough. She began to plan that children might have a full and happy life, wherever they were. *Plus flamme que femme*, a great writer described her—'more flame than woman'—and she burned with a passionate determination that children everywhere should have their rights.

The flame began to consume her, for she was never well. Her constant journeyings throughout Europe racked her thin body, though they never touched her spirit. In 1923, four years after the Fund had begun, she slowly climbed a mountain which looked down on Geneva. Here, in neutral Switzerland, the League of Nations was beginning its task of peace-making. Through jealousies and national pride it was to fail—but on the mountain that day Eglantine Jebb wrote down the notes of a children's charter. It was one thing the League was to give the world which would live long after its own unhappy ending.

'The child must be protected . . . the child must be cared for . . . must be given the means for its normal development . . . the child that is hungry must be fed; the child that is sick must be nursed; the child that is . . . handicapped must be helped; the maladjusted child must be re-educated; the orphan and the waif must be sheltered and succoured . . . the child must be the first to receive relief . . . the child must enjoy the full benefits provided by social welfare . . . must receive a training . . . must be brought up in the consciousness that its talents must be devoted to the service of its fellow-men'.

Her first notes were less full, but they were the basis of her *Declaration of the Rights of the Child*. The following year, 1924, the Declaration was commended by the League of Nations to all member countries as a guide for laws relating to child welfare. Revised in 1948, it remains the charter of the Save the Children Fund.

As she travelled round Europe, increasingly unwell, she saw for herself that here and there relief was giving place to planning for the future. King Boris of Bulgaria himself drove the train which took her to see new model villages, one of them called Xheba, an Albanian attempt at her own name. She saw a clinic for blind children in Greece, a new children's hospital in Jugoslavia, the beginnings of practical service in Britain that was to lead to clubs, playgroups and residential homes in her own country.

In 1928, back in her beloved Geneva, she died. The flame which had consumed her had lit countless others. It brought light and hope. It burned away evil and useless things. Today it flares up in lands still unborn when she died. It illuminates the greatest of human rights—the rights of the child.

25

Annie Ruth Jiagge

THE BLUE TRIANGLE

Mrs Jiagge lists her hobbies as 'gardening and poultry'. She must have had little enough time for them. What other people often regard as spare-time interests, almost hobbies, have been for her a consuming passion. Long before the mid-sixties heard the cry of 'Women's Liberation' Mrs Jiagge was deeply involved in the struggle for women's rights. She did not see her part in this campaign as marching in protest or waving placards. She was at the centre of the movement, at the place where decisions are made.

Even to many who know little of the position of women in African society the achievements of Annie Jiagge of Ghana must seem remarkable. As, indeed, they are.

Daughter of a Presbyterian minister who was stationed at Lomé, in Togo, she went to the famous Achimota Teacher Training College near Accra in Ghana in 1934. Here the name of Dr Kwegyir Aggrey, its vice-principal and most famous figure, was deeply revered. The Achimota crest devised by Aggrey, consisting of the black and white notes of the piano—'on which', in Aggrey's words, 'you can only play real tunes when black and white are used together'—was significant for her from the beginning. If she believed in the rightful place of her own black nation, the Gold Coast as it then was, she firmly held to Aggrey's internationalism. A factor in her upbringing was her own father's period of theological study in Germany.

For nearly two years she taught at Keta Presbyterian school and was then appointed its headmistress. The sea washed away part of its buildings and Annie Jiagge set out to raise money to put up even better buildings for its four hundred girls by touring the country with a musical play performed by the girls.

In 1946, in her thirties, she realised an ambition to study in Britain. Her mother found the money for this further education, first at the London School of Economics and the following year at Lincoln's Inn.

Two or three streams of concern came together at this point in her life. The Gold Coast government gave her a scholarship to study social welfare institutions run by local Councils in Britain, and to report on how they might be adapted to conditions in her own country. Bishop Bell, of Chichester, appointed her with three other black students to visit Germany, exchanging ideas and concerns with post-war German students. Still more important, she was elected a member of the World

Y.W.C.A. Executive. With members of this movement she toured Europe, and began to build up her wide knowledge of other countries and her increasing sense of belonging to the whole world Church.

For the next ten years the Y.W.C.A. was to have a great part of her time and the famous 'blue triangle' houses and headquarters saw her in many parts of the world. In 1951 she was in the Middle East; in 1953 in India; in 1955 in Britain, when she was elected a World Vice-President; and in 1959 in Mexico.

These, however, were busy journeys fitted with difficulty into a very full life in her own country. As a barrister she worked in chambers in Accra but between 1957 and 1961 she was appointed a magistrate, a circuit judge and finally a High Court Judge.

During the whole period of the Nkrumah regime she maintained a reputation of integrity and incorruptibility and, as soon as the Liberation Committee took over from the ousted president, she was appointed head of a commission—the Jiagge Commission—to enquire into the financial situation of a considerable number of people who had achieved eminence under Nkrumah.

At the same time as she was giving service to women and girls within her own country and throughout the world through the Y.W.C.A. she was also deeply involved in the World Council of Churches. Present at the inaugural assembly in Amsterdam—one of the very few laymen who were there—she quickly became a member of the Commission on Laity. The Ghana government also appointed her its representative on the United Nations Commission on the status of women.

In a world where the white countries still all too easily patronise the black nations of Africa and Asia, women like Mrs Justice Jiagge of Ghana challenge our complacency. With a world-consciousness and a social conscience born out of Christian faith and compassion, she represents a host of women who have taken their full place in Church and society.

DAWN OVER ROME

'May you one day be Pope in Rome!'

The Roncalli family made the old jest easily, amidst the tears and laughter, breaking the sudden reserve that came over them as they looked at Angelo in his new black cassock, his head shaved in the tonsure fringed by black hair. He was only fourteen but he had set his foot on the road to the priesthood. Born in the little village of Sotto il Monte—'under the mountain'—in northern Italy, he had moved from one school to another. Walking further each time, until he went to the cathedral city of Bergamo to the seminary. Now, that Saturday in 1895, he had begun the life he had always longed for. To his parents and school-fellows it seemed likely to lead only to the care of some mountain parish like Sotto il Monte. The jest was no more than that customary ice-breaking salutation with which all boys were greeted on such a day. Its absurdity was a proper reminder of the need for humility.

Nothing would have suited Angelo Roncalli better, as he looked to the future, than the care of peasants like his own family. He too was a peasant, and to the end of his life he would never quite lose the rough northern accent which made the cultured Romans raise their eyebrows when they first heard it. He loved people, and especially simple people. More deeply, he loved God. He had no desire greater than to serve people wherever God might call him.

It is all too easy, especially for Protestants who seldom understand the depth of devotion in men like Roncalli, to see statesmen such as he only as public figures, exercising authority, promulgating decisions, caught up in the politics of a worldly-wise ecclesiastical organisation. Roncalli did indeed become something of an international statesman, long before he became Pope. But to read his personal diary, *The Journal of a Soul*, is to find a man truly saintly, utterly committed to God, echoing Martin Luther's resolve that because he would be busier than ever he must spend yet more time in prayer.

Throughout his life he never slept more than four hours each night. The last hours before sleep and the hours before dawn were given to God, whom he sought not through formal phrases but through the Bible, meditation and prayer.

It is against this unremitting search for the will of God that his busy public life must be seen.

At the college of the Appolinare in Rome he showed himself a brilliant student, breaking off in the midst of his studies to do his year of statutory army service. It was no surprise to his tutors that when he was ordained and due to leave the seminary Roncalli was appointed assistant to the cardinal-bishop of Bergamo. For fifteen years he was able to serve in his beloved northern land, near to his own home. He learned much as the bishop's assistant in all his duties, but perhaps most of all when a strike broke out in the Bergamo factories. The aristocratic bishop, Count Radini Tedeschi, instead of siding with the factory-owners, preached from his cathedral pulpit in favour of the workers and moved amongst the strikers with Roncalli at his side. With great gifts of administration and brilliant scholarship the young priest learned afresh that the most important things in the world were people, and that ordinary people were most important of all.

In the First World War he served as hospital orderly, saving most of his meagre thousand lire per month salary to begin a hostel for students in Bergamo, already planned in his mind, when the war was over. He saw worse troubles ahead for Italy than the war itself, and was proved right. In the hostel the conflicting ideologies of Communism and the Fascism that was to lift Mussolini to power were both in conflict with religious faith. He was never more at home than in the debates of these young men.

A great congress at Bergamo, when he had charge of all the administration, really launched him into public life. He was appointed from Bergamo to Rome, to a post which kept him moving throughout Europe from the Baltic to the Balkans. It was a task which demonstrated his gift for languages, his ability with officials and, above all, his tact and understanding in promoting peace out of often divisive situations.

It was this gift of peace-making which led to his appointment to one of the trickiest posts the Vatican had to fill. In 1925 he was sent as Apostolic Visitor to Bulgaria—a sort of ambassador from the Vatican to a country divided between Catholics and Orthodox. The first Sunday he announced in his sermon that he would begin learning Bulgarian the next morning, and that he would try and visit every Catholic in the country. Both promises were taken as mere showmanship—but both were fulfilled as far as he was able. Not only through the towns and villages near Sofia, but by cart, pony and on foot he visited remote communities, often hungry, often in danger from brigands, often sleeping in village inns and mountain huts. Before he left he had endeared himself to Catholic, Orthodox and Muslim, and they wept at his going.

The next appointment was more difficult still—Apostolic Delegate to Greece and Turkey. Under Kemal 'Ataturk', Turkey had become officially an atheistic state, where even Roncalli had to wear civilian clothes for the first time since he had been a farm-boy in Sotto il Monte. During this appointment Greece was invaded by the Italians when the Second World War broke out. Roncalli's position was unenviable and the Greeks made no secret of their suspicions that he was a spy. In fact, his 'spying' was mainly of the humanitarian kind—information about refugees, 'disappearances' and the desperate need of the Greek people for food and medical services. By his mediation with the British on the one hand, and the Germans on the other, he managed to have 400,000 tons of grain imported, mainly for the refugees, many of whom were starving.

The war over, he had his most demanding posting of all. He became Papal Nuncio to France, the senior diplomatic appointment of the Vatican. Peace-making here taxed all his resources. The Catholic Church was unpopular in a country which was largely anti-clerical, and priests and bishops were accused of collaborating with the Nazis and the Vichy government. Darting in and out of bookshops by the Seine, known to the little shop-keepers as a friend, expertly mixing with ambassadors and the French government, he bridged gaps and exercised a ministry of reconciliation which was acknowledged by the President of the Republic when he was summoned back to Italy in 1951.

He was at last going home and, at the age of seventy, nothing could have given him greater joy. In Venice, where he had been appointed cardinal-archbishop, every gondola, launch and river-taxi in the city turned out to welcome him. They turned out again to wish him 'good luck' in 1958 when he went to Rome to share in the election of a new pope. His best luck would be to return quickly, he told them, and they had every reason to believe him. He had opened his palace to all who came. He had given away all but a tiny amount of his salary. He had refused to have a personal gondola and travelled on the river buses. When his light went on at four o'clock in the morning his people knew he was praying for them.

But Roncalli did not return.

Instead, he was elected Pope after ten ballots.

A 'caretaker pope', said the world's press. 'An old man, nearly eighty, too old to make any difference!'

He quickly proved them wrong. His first decision was to be called pope John. No predecessor had been called John for six centuries, for the last had been a rebel and a misfit. But John the Apostle was Roncalli's beloved master in spiritual things, his Gospel was more often read than any other.

Astonishing headlines rolled quickly from the world's presses. *Pope John holds first-ever press conference.* He shared his ideas with five hundred journalists, and some of the ideas were revolutionary. *Pope raises Vatican wages*—after he asked an electrician if he could live on what he earned. *Pope creates twenty-three new cardinals.* Younger men were needed in the Church's councils, including Africans and Asians. *Pope visits prisoners.* He would not be imprisoned himself within the Vatican. Visiting the gaols, he refused to go down the red-carpeted corridors and sought out the places he was not expected to see. *Pope escapes*—giving his outriders and detectives the slip he went to tea with an old priest-friend. Staid conservatism was being swept away. To love God meant that one loved men—not from a distance, from behind the curtains of protocol, but close at hand.

On Christmas Day, 1961, he made his most dramatic headlines. *Pope Summons New Ecumenical Council.* It was, apart from an abortive one in the 1880's, the first since the middle ages.

The Council began on 11th October, 1962. On 3rd June, 1963, Pope John XXIII died, while it was still in session. The things for which he had laboured all his life dominated its work.

The Church must come out from behind its high walls. It must face the problems of poverty, race and the lack of human rights. Church services must be held in the language of the people. The Bible must be at the centre of every home and every life. The debates swung between his own two poles—God and people.

Most startling of all changes, however, was Pope John's loving welcome to those whom his predecessors had all called 'heretics'. Protestants—'Evangelicals' as they are called in continental Europe—came to the Council as 'observers' and found themselves sharing in its discussions. Protestant and Catholic discovered that the vision of God might be coloured by the angle from which one looked, but that the voice of God came clearly to both. As Pope John had heard it that Voice called men to deeper love, a more profound understanding of each other and a shared concern for the poor of the earth.

27
Toyohiko Kagawa

THE TRAITOR

Kagawa has been one of the formative figures of the Christian Church in this century. Like many other reformers, because he was a score of years ahead of his contemporaries, he seemed to be set on betraying the things many of them valued most. The old religion of his family and nation; the church-based organisation of the Christian faith to which he turned; the materialistic security of a nation newly emerging into the twentieth century; then, at last, the power of his own empire, rooted in the worship of its emperor . . . all these things, which so many cherished, he turned from and denounced.

For this reason he was himself denounced, imprisoned, and threatened with death.

Yet because he was a true revolutionary, building more firmly than he destroyed, and much more because his life matched his Christian faith, he remains one of the outstanding Christians of the twentieth century.

Born in 1882, at a time when modern Japan was coming to life, he was the son of a wealthy industrialist and the *geisha* woman for whom his father had deserted his country wife. On his father's death he was taken to the ancestral home at Awa—a precocious, introvert child, bullied by his grandmother and school-fellows and more than once tempted to suicide.

Hope came to him only when he was sent into the care of a wealthy uncle in Kobe, to attend the school where his brother had gone before him. Here, from American missionaries engaged to teach the boys English, he heard for the first time the story of Jesus. The wonder of the crucifixion story transformed him. On the mat in the missionary's study he made his first prayer and committed himself to Christ.

'O God', he prayed, 'make me like Jesus Christ!'

Rejection came swiftly when he told his uncle that he wished to become a Christian minister. He was turned out of the house. Rejection came again when he refused to join in the army drill compulsory for all school-boys. He was beaten senseless by the drill-sergeant. At college in Tokyo, a year or two later, he was attacked once more and nearly killed by his fellow-students for denouncing the war in which Japan was engaged. Dragging himself to his feet he prayed for his persecutors—and one of them was to share, a few years afterwards, in his ordination.

Kobe, at that time, was already a growing industrial city with great dockyards where the workers lived in appalling conditions in the slums of the Shinkawa district across the river from the respectable township. It was in the township itself that the Christian church was established. But Kagawa, already reading French and German as well as he read English, and marked out by his professors for eventual leadership in the life of the small but growing Christian community, turned his back on respectability.

On Christmas Day, 1909, he crossed the Bridge of the Singing Cicada, pushing a handcart with his few belongings—mostly books—and rented an empty hut in the slums of Shinkawa. The first night he shared his hut with a depraved alcoholic and the next day he counted fourteen fights. Taken for a police spy, a madman, a rich man's son escaping the police, he slowly established himself as a figure to be reckoned with. He preached twice a day, opened his door to all who sought shelter, rented more huts alongside his own with money sent to him by well-wishers and turned them into a communal home for anyone who sought his help. Long into the night he wrote, using magazine pages for his manuscript-paper, covering the print with black ink characters.

Three things changed his life at this point. He married, and brought his wife to live in the slums. He spent a year studying in the United States. And his first novel, dealing with slum-life, *Across the Death-Line*, was published. It sold at a prodigious rate, and swept his name into the headlines. The book was a protest against the degradations of the slums. But his time in America had changed him from a protester into a social reformer. He set out to bring hope to the workers of Japan.

Inevitably he clashed with authority. The first time was when he led the workers of Shinkawa to the Town Hall to demand better wages and working conditions. Flung into prison he was released just in time to prevent the dock-workers from surging into the shipyards to wreak havoc on ships and docks. His action established him not only as a leader but as a man of integrity. Things began to change for the workers. The first Trades Unions came into existence and under Kagawa's influence there began a new struggle for the rural workers of the neglected countryside with eventual success.

By the middle of the 1920s he was the best-selling author in Japan. Poems, novels, social treatises, books on politics or religion—whenever a new book was published queues formed outside the bookshops.

When the great earthquake destroyed so much of Tokyo and Yokohama in 1923 Kagawa went immediately with a boatload of food, clothes and blankets. To his astonishment he was made a member of a committee, which included the very industrialists against whom he had been fighting, commissioned to replan and rebuild the city. The earthquake had destroyed Tokyo's slums. By this time Kagawa's authority was sufficient to persuade the government to produce a plan for the complete demolition and rebuilding of the slum-areas, not only in Tokyo but in all Japan's major cities. His influence was immense.

But, in the 1930s, a change came to the nation. The militarists achieved almost absolute power.

First they declared war on China—and were humiliated because Kagawa undertook a tour across that stricken country, apologising for his nation's action. In 1941, with the bombing of the American fleet in Pearl Harbour, at the very moment when Kagawa was leading a prayer-meeting that war might be averted, hostilities broke out between Japan and America.

The next years were the most desperate Kagawa had ever known. His church closed, his books banned, he himself forbidden to preach and at times forced into hiding, he was denounced as a traitor. At the same time the Japanese propagandists broadcast alleged denunciations of America in his name. By the time the war ended, with the horrific bombing of Hiroshima, he was believed in America to be a traitor who had renounced his faith and his friends.

Yet it was he who finally penetrated to General MacArthur's headquarters and helped persuade the general to a policy of peace-making which, in a remarkably short time, was to lead to new nation-building and hope. In the years that followed he organised relief, settlements, medical centres, public works.

Behind all this immense programme of social renewal was the power of an overwhelming, simple Christian faith. Christian belief underlay all his social and political programmes. Faith kept him going when, racked with eye-disease and ravaged by the remnants of tuberculosis, he preached every Sunday and organised missions year after year throughout the land. The growing materialism of his nation he regarded with anxiety and horror from his small, simple house with its minimal furniture and its rows of books on packing-case shelves.

To the end his proclamation remained the same.

The whole gospel—for the whole man.

THE FLAG IN THE HILLS

Kawl Khuma, his parents called him—'Overcomer of the Universe'. It was a large title for a small boy born into the Lushai Hills at the end of the last century.

The Lushai people, on the frontiers of India in the hills to the north of Burma, were isolated from most of the changes beginning to affect India itself. They remained spirit-worshippers, and continued the old farming practice of burning down the bamboo forest, planting rice, and then after harvest moving on while the forest closed in again. They had scarcely given up their head-hunting activities when Kawl was born.

Yet this boy, longing for education, trudged across the hills to Aijal, his nearest town, and earned enough coppers cleaning soldiers' cooking pots to pay his way at primary school. Seeking further education, as few even of the primary scholars did, he was one of the first class in the Lushai hills to pass the Class 8 English examination.

At Aijal, however, he gained more than a sound basic education. In the mission hall in the bazaar he heard the story of Jesus for the first time, and became a baptised Christian, confirming his faith by tramping back across the hills to win his mother for Christ before he went on with his studies. It was this new sense of commitment to others that decided his choice of work. He became a dispenser, first in Diarkhai village and a year later in a new mission dispensary at Aijal—the town that was to figure so often in his story.

Aged 19, he got married. His wife, Khuangi, was chosen by his family, in the traditional Lushai way. Then came disaster. The dispensary closed and the missionary returned to England. Kawl took a job in the Public Works Department, finding himself caught up in the all-too-normal corruption of petty officials. He divorced his wife and took another woman to live with him—and was shocked when his actions cut him off from membership of the church.

In that situation Kawl might well have ended, not even overcoming himself, much less the universe, if there had not been a spiritual revival in the hills in which he was caught up and changed once more.

One result of his changed life was that he took his wife back, and re-married her. Another was an urgent longing to witness for Christ, so that for the time being he gave up normal work altogether and set off amongst the villages with a pack on his back. A third result was that, with a few friends, he formed a Christian community. They called themselves the 'Soldiers of the Cross' and even had a uniform—a khaki coat with red flashes on the breast-pockets. There it might have ended again, with a useful Christian group of village preachers, if a shopkeeper had not made a passing remark.

'That uniform of yours', said Dohnuna, 'looks very much like the Salvation Army to me!'

The name caught their imagination. Where could they find out more? Simla? But that was hundreds of miles away. Nevertheless Kawl and a friend set off for Calcutta and then across the Indian plains and up the foothills of the Himalayas to the summer capital of the Indian government. It was a providential time to arrive. A Salvation Army meeting was in progress in the bazaar—and Kawl imagined the cornet, the drums and the flags winding across his far-away hills. There was an exhibition of work done by the tribes amongst whom the Army worked. More than this, there was a welcome from Commissioner Booth-Tucker, the head of India's Salvation Army.

Almost before he knew what was happening Kawl Khuma was travelling on to the Salvation Army training-school in Bombay. By 1917, still a young man under thirty, he was back in his beloved, cool Lushai Hills, a Salvationist. The flag had arrived in the hills—or, at any rate, the story of the flag. There was still a great deal of 'overcoming' ahead.

The Indian Government, uneasy about the Lushais with their head-hunting history, wanted them disturbed as little as possible. Only two missions were allowed to work in Lushai country, and the Salvation Army was not one of them. After a while restrictions were lifted, and a 'boom march' went on up and down the valleys—two cornets, the flag, the drums and two preachers. New songs caught the imagination of these music-loving hill-folk. Then once more the restrictions were invoked, and Kawl Khuma spent his time living in Aijal, translating Salvation Army books, the Articles of War and the songs, into the tongue of his own people. Another period of freedom followed, until other Christians made objections that the Army was stealing their people. Once again the government stepped in and, though no attempt was made to get rid of Kawl and his hundreds of 'soldiers', it was not until 1928 that the work was properly restarted, openly and without restriction. The following year the first eight Lushai cadets were commissioned after training, as officers amongst their own people.

Religious by temperament, the Lushai people found much in the vigour, the music and the gospel-presentation of the Salvationists which attracted them. Kawl Khuma moved up from rank to rank, though he never moved away from concern for his own people. For twenty years he was their inspiration and their leader, deeply loved by them. Not until 1949, after a visit to Britain, was he removed. That was to become a pioneer in Silchar, amongst the Cachar people, and a little later to head up advance work in Manipur State.

He had seen the 1939-46 war come and go, flowing amongst the Burmese hills and the plains of Assam. His people had been caught up in it and, like their once head-hunting Naga neighbours, had worked as stretcher-bearers. Through it all the Salvationists stood firmly by their faith.

When Kawl retired in 1956 he left a soldiers' roll of four hundred Salvationists. Not that retirement meant ease. In the years that followed he visited every corps in the Lushai hills, some of them many times. No greater honour could be given him than the 'Order of the Founder' and this he received in 1966—a man who truly overcame.

29
Martin Luther King

'I HAVE A DREAM TODAY!'

Martin Luther King had no intention of being a minister like his father. Not because he had any criticisms of such a profession. Indeed, he had the greatest respect for his father and the work he did. He himself was a devout Christian. But he was also, even as a youth, dedicated to the advancement of his own people, and it seemed likely to him that he would serve them better in some other way. As a lawyer, perhaps . . . certainly as a speaker of some sort.

His parents' home was comfortable and cultured. On the face of things it did not seem likely they would suffer much from discrimination or hardship. Yet as a schoolboy Martin was forbidden to play with the white children he had scuffled with as a toddler. There was nearly a riot when his school-fellows were turned out of the seats of a bus retained for whites. On a long-distance train in the north he was allowed to sit in the dining-car but the attendant drew a curtain round him so that he would not offend his fellow-diners, all whites.

At college he suddenly saw that a minister had opportunities of leadership and service denied to almost everyone else. He could no longer resist the call which had been growing within him. He knew that God wanted him in the ministry. How and where he would be used must wait on events.

The 'where' came as clearly as his call to the pastor's office. Though his young wife Coretta would have preferred the North, with its freer society, he felt a commitment to the Southern states, where Negroes suffered the bitterest humiliations. With a high scholastic record, and a reputation as a preacher of great ability, he was invited to Dexter Avenue Baptist Church in Montgomery, Alabama.

His congregation included many doctors, lawyers, professors, teachers, men and women of intelligence and standing in the black community. To the whites the blacks were 'trash'. All Negroes might not sit in white men's cafes, worship in white churches, earn white men's wages, ride in the seats reserved for whites in the buses, or send their children to white schools.

When the Federal government passed its famous desegregation law, giving black children the right to attend white schools, the southern states refused to obey the new statute. To protect themselves against Negro intransigence as a result of their refusal they set up white 'Citizens' Councils'.

Within a matter of weeks the sense of injustice and resentment threatened to boil over into violence.

But the storm in Montgomery broke for quite another reason. On 1st December 1955 a quiet, inoffensive black dressmaker, Rosa Parkes, sat in a bus seat reserved for whites and refused to move as the bus filled. Inevitably she was arrested.

Dr King immediately went into action. Until then it had seemed to him that the way forward to a fuller life for black people was by patient argument and firm pressure on the authorities. The 'Citizens' Councils' had changed all that and King had heard the imminent rumblings of a storm of violence. He himself was opposed to all violence, whether by his own people or by white citizens. He would be opposed to it throughout his life. Like his great hero, Mahatma Gandhi, he believed that effective change in society could only be brought about by non-violent means.

This did not mean, however, that he was content to sit back and do nothing. With other Negro leaders he immediately urged a boycott of the buses as long as blacks were refused the right to sit where they liked. The City Council needed the money from the buses; blacks needed them to get to work, often many miles away from where they lived. Nevertheless, as King and his wife Coretta watched the bus-stop outside their house the morning after Rosa Parkes was arrested they saw blacks walking, cycling, riding on carts . . . but none on the buses.

The boycott lasted for three hundred and eighty-two days.

Just before Christmas 1956 the City Council gave way. Black people might sit where they liked. Dr King had won his first non-violent victory.

But he had already learned the cost of leadership. Six weeks after the boycott began, he was arrested. Four days later his house was bombed. A huge crowd of Negroes quickly surged around it with bars, stones and bottles, determined to avenge their beloved minister. King calmed their outraged tempers and sent them home. The white citizens did not thank him for it; they would have preferred a riot and an excuse to teach the 'black trash' a lesson.

The success of the boycott brought another danger to King—a danger to his soul, as he saw it. He became a household name, known in north and south.

Invitations to pastorates all over the country reached him. He was pressed to undertake lecture tours—even offered a professorship at a white university. This was the moment of his greatest temptation. Yet he saw himself as a minister first and a Negro leader second; not at all as a 'hero' on exhibition. For the time being he remained at Montgomery, though in 1959 he accepted his only other pastorate, in his home town of Atlanta.

Nonetheless, his influence was assured. In 1957 he founded the Southern Christian Leadership Conference. A new, significant phrase was born, and taken up all over America. 'Civil Rights' was a crisp statement of his aims. The right to live where one wished, to full education, to vote, to citizenship. He had a simplicity of style and a lambent fire in his oratory which began to run throughout the southern states.

It was the Prayer Pilgrimage which made him a national figure.

On 17th May 1959, thirty-nine thousand pilgrims from thirty states, whites as well as blacks, converged on Washington. There was no violence, no hostility, no demonstration other than the seemingly endless throng moving towards the Lincoln Memorial. From its steps a great array of speakers addressed the crowd, but it was King whose magnetism made the day memorable. He demanded rights for all the oppressed, white as well as black. Rights, not privileges, he emphasised.

Before the rally was over he had become the acknowledged leader of sixteen million Negroes throughout the land.

Soon after the Pilgrimage he was invited to visit Ghana to attend the independence celebrations. His visit confirmed his estimate of the capabilities of black people. Back in the States he was in his old, sad world.

Within a few weeks of his return he was arrested. It was a token gesture which almost backfired. Fined, to show the contempt of the white municipality for a black hero, he refused to pay the fine. He announced that he would prefer to go to jail. The police were suddenly scared as a huge crowd collected outside the courtroom. They *dared* not take him to jail. In consternation the police-chief himself paid the fine and set him free.

A fortnight later when he sat signing copies of his first book in a Harlem store, a psychopathic woman pulled a long knife from her dress and stabbed him, narrowly missing his heart. It was by the narrowest of margins that he did not die.

After a visit to India he came back to his new pastorate in Atlanta. Here a new chapter in non-violence began. A group of college students took their place in a white restaurant and refused to move. 'We shall sit here until we're served, or until you throw us out!'

A new technique, and a new word, was born. 'Sit-ins' swiftly caught on. In stores, supermarkets, cinemas, theatres, libraries all over the country young people sat until, unresisting, they were dragged out. Naturally King joined the movement. Inevitably, too, he was arrested.

This time his arrest had a result which shook America and certainly helped to change its history.

1960 was the year of the Presidential election, and Nixon and Kennedy were campaigning across the country. At Kennedy's headquarters someone told him of King's arrest. He walked across the room, asked for a long-distance phone-call and to her amazement Coretta King found herself talking to the Presidential candidate. He assured her that he would do what he could for her husband.

The next day Dr King was set free.

Within hours the story was in every headline and every news-bulletin. There seems little doubt that that phone-call helped to carry John F. Kennedy into the Presidential chair. He was to become one of King's warmest supporters, though he was assassinated before he could sign the Civil Rights Bill which he championed. It was his successor, Lyndon B. Johnson, who signed it in his place.

Four more times King was arrested and freed again before the most memorable march of all, in June 1963.

A quarter of a million people marched on Washington, amongst them sixty thousand whites. It was the most peaceful Civil Rights demonstration of all time—and it produced from Dr King perhaps the most remarkable of all his speeches. It was not a short speech, but the crowd was utterly still. Then came his peroration.

'I have a dream today . . .'

Over and over again he repeated the phrase, and the crowd shouted, and then wept, as the words rolled on.

'I have a dream that my four little children will one day live in a nation where they will not be judged by the colour of their skin but by their character . . .

'I have a dream today.

'I have a dream that the state of Alabama will one day be transformed . . . little black boys and girls and little white boys and girls will walk together as sisters and brothers . . .

'I have a dream today . . .

'I have a dream that one day every valley shall be exalted, every hill made low . . . the glory of the Lord shall be revealed and all flesh shall see it together.

'I have a dream today . . .'

On 2nd July, 1964, President Johnson signed the Civil Rights Bill, with Martin Luther King and other Negro leaders by his side.

In that same year he was awarded the Nobel Prize for Peace.

Two more years went by, busier than ever. There were always causes to be fought for, injustices to be put right. In April, 1967, it was the garbage-workers of Memphis who were appealing for better conditions of work. King went to Memphis to join their march.

Martin Luther King

On 4th April, walking onto his hotel balcony to breathe the fresh air after a long conference, he was shot dead.

He was not yet thirty-nine when he died.

30

Frank C. Laubach

THE SILENT BILLION

It was Dr Laubach's own name for them—the silent thousand million whose number has grown with the years since his campaigns began, despite all his own successes and those of others like him. Silent because, compared with those who can read and therefore write, they have no voice.

Yet, all over the world, their voice is growing.

Men, women and children are learning to read.

It is a process that has its dangers. Those who have just learned to read will read whatever comes their way. They have little discernment. They are the prey of shrewd political agitators, unscrupulous advertisers, purveyors of pornography and trash. The fact that they have learned to read puts a new burden on those who can write for simple men.

So, all over the world, the Church is giving new attention to literature. Training writers to provide simple, useful books and journalists to produce Christian magazines and newspapers. Training translators to turn the Bible and great Christian books, new and old, into the idiom of those to whom reading has opened the gates of a new world.

Despite its dangers, the possibilities for good, for those who have learned to read, are greater than ever before.

No man in our time has done more to open the gates into this new world than Frank Laubach, missionary-extraordinary and pioneer of a method that revolutionised literacy techniques.

In 1915 he sailed half-way round the world to what was described as 'one of the toughest jobs on earth' with his young bride, Effa Seely. At the age of twenty-one they landed on Mindanao, in the Philippines. Pioneering was in his blood, even if it was a few generations back. The Laubachs of Pennsylvania were descended from Germans who had landed in America when it was still a British colony, in 1738. Frank's father told him how, when he was still a boy, the first log cabin still stood in Fishing Creek. The pioneering spirit had been stirred in young Frank when a government official visited his school at Benton, seeking students to teach in the Philippines. Too young then to respond, Frank Laubach later became a Presbyterian missionary and followed the two students who had gone from his own school.

The Laubachs' first disappointment came quickly—and there were to be many more. Fighting was still continuing between the Moros, the indigenous inhabitants of Lanao, and the United States, who had recently taken over the islands from the Spaniards. Instead of going to his appointed station, he had to settle down to the life of a missionary teacher in Mindanao and then in Manila. The disappointment lasted a long time. Not until 1929 was he permitted by the authorities to move to Manao, to the Moro country.

Frustration was immediate. The Muslim Moros would not listen to his preaching. His only companion (his wife was not allowed to join him) was a drunken American who scoffed at him. By the end of the first month he had almost given up. Then, sitting on Signal Hill looking out to sea, he seemed to hear a voice. 'You have failed because you don't really love these Moros. You feel superior to them, and you show it in all you do. Listen to them. Study their Koran as you hope they will study the Bible.' In that awful moment of self-revelation Laubach was transformed. He himself wrote afterwards: 'In that terrible, wonderful hour on Signal Hill I became colour-blind.' From that moment it never mattered to him what was the colour of a man's skin. The only thing that did matter was that God loved those to whom he had sent this missionary with his new vision and understanding.

At the bottom of Signal Hill he met a group of Muslim priests, watching him suspiciously. He stopped and spoke to them, asking if they would tell him about their own holy book, the Koran. Next morning a whole crowd of them arrived at his house. He could hardly get a word into the conversation. He had broken the barrier—but he could not yet speak Maranao, the local language. It was essential to find a teacher.

The teacher appeared—a convicted murderer, sentenced to twenty years' imprisonment, whose sentence had been drastically shortened. It did not matter to Laubach. The murderer was a good teacher, and soon afterwards they were joined by Galia, a Philippino missionary and his wife. The trouble with Maranao was that it was solely a spoken language. You could not get people to read the Bible in a language that had never been written down. This was Laubach's next task. At the end of six weeks he and Galia had written down thirteen hundred words.

Now the problem was to get illiterate people to read—to make them *want* to read.

Throughout his life Dr Laubach has been certain that God has guided every decision, every step. Never was he more sure than in these next few months. A trader gave them a disused drink-shop to use as a school. A derelict cinema, built when the American soldiers were at Lanao, became a church. A friend sold them a printing-press for a tenth of its value, and with it came a good Philippino printer, Silvino. The press was far too heavy to stand on the floor of the building they had chosen for their printing-shop. In the mountains there was no concrete, nor any means of making it. Laubach and Galia began to rip up the wooden floor in the hope that the ground below might be reasonably firm. Underneath, they found a concrete base exactly the size they needed for the press!

So far, so good. The Moro language was written down. The missionaries could read it—but no one else could do so. What then?

'Let's print a newspaper,!' exclaimed Laubach.

They did so, laboriously setting it up by hand in Arabic, the tongue of the Muslim priests, and in Roman-script Maranao. When it came off the press, its print still wet, the priests began to read. 'Chiefs will tell the stories of the Moro people . . . this paper will give the prices of corn, rice, beans, cloth, silk, brass and gold articles . . .' The priest read the Arabic; Galia read the Maranao script.

'But it says the same thing!' cried the excited people. 'You must teach us to read our own language. We want to read the newspaper ourselves.'

Once the will to learn was there teaching the Moros proved very much easier than Laubach had expected. Following the priests and the chiefs came the ordinary tribesmen—villagers, farmers, outlaws. One thousand five hundred people learned to read in a month. Helpers came too. In the crowded schoolroom at Lanao fifty-one young men volunteered for the task. Now, however, Laubach had bad news. Mission boards were retrenching. Income in the U.S.A. was down, and there was no more money to pay the assistants. The people were aghast. One of the young men said that he had taught forty-one women and seventy-one men to read in the past month. Surely the campaign could not stop now! If Laubach had no answer Kakai Dagalangit, the chief of southern Lanao, had an answer of his own.

'This must not stop. Literacy is the hope of our people. Everybody who learns has got to teach. If he doesn't, I'll kill him!'

He meant what he said. As he uttered the threat Laubach had an inspiration which was to prove one of the most significant ideas in literacy-teaching history.

'Each one, teach one!'

'Everyone who learns must teach. You cannot have another lesson until you have taught someone else the one you have learned yourself'.

A new revolution had begun.

Laubach's 'each one teach one' method caught the imagination of the Philippine government. The five years that followed were the busiest he had ever known. The idea spread everywhere, and Laubach was in constant demand throughout the area. After one demonstration the President of the Philippines asserted: 'I'm going home to teach my cook to read before I have my dinner!'

Requests for information began to come in from all over the world. 'Two people out of every three in the world cannot read,' Laubach told his helpers. 'And we've begun something that can change the face of the world.' In 1935 Laubach set off for America after one of the most triumphant farewells ever seen in the Philippines. He stopped in India and Egypt on the way home. Using his simplified reading charts, the basis of his new reading method, he proved that his idea worked in other places besides the Pacific.

There were two results of his visit to the United States. One was that a new committee was set up on which most of the larger missionary societies were represented—the World Literacy Committee. The other, Laubach himself became the travelling representative of the committee.

The next twenty years sound like the diary of a man who could never stand still. 'Honolulu . . . Central Africa . . . India . . . Brazil . . . East Africa . . . Guatemala . . . Jamaica.' Every year he met thousands of new literacy workers. The work spread everywhere. The Laubach charts appeared in shanty town, bush village, desert cities. Each one still taught another. Never in all this did Frank Laubach forget that he was a missionary. The primary reason for all his effort was not merely that men should read, but that they should read the good news.

The world can never forget that it was Dr Frank Laubach, more than any man in the twentieth century, who began to widen the vision of those who could see but not read.

PILGRIMAGE

'Blessed art thou, O Lord . . .'

The little Jewish boy grew up with thanksgiving all round him. 'Blessed art Thou, O Lord our God, King of the Universe, who removest sleep from mine eyes . . .' 'Blessed art Thou . . . for food, for rain, for holidays, for books, for work' . . . for everything that life held. The Lipsons were a thankful family, but most of all they were full of gratitude that the Lord God had so ordered life that they should be part of His chosen people—scattered, persecuted, exiled on account of their sins, but nevertheless the people of God.

Little Eric was not allowed to twist thanksgiving into unwholesome pride, however, and still less into contempt for men of other faiths. His father was minister at the synagogue in Kentish Town, London, and their home was next door. Not only that, his father was himself descended from a long line of Jewish Rabbis. The synagogue was as familiar to Eric as his own home. He began to learn Hebrew when he was six years old and the words of the Scripture not only flowed over him day by day, as it was read at home, but became part of his very being. To Eric, there was no such thing as 'too much religion'.

Though he was withdrawn from Christian religious instruction at school, it was by no means an unliberal household. The New Testament was not proscribed reading, and one of his prized treasures was a beautifully bound Bible with both Testaments.

How then did Eric Lipson find in Christianity the fulfilment of ideals and purposes he had grown up with inside Judaism?

Partly the generosity of thought in his own home, no doubt, where there was not only no antipathy to the New Testament but an openness to Christian friends, even to Christians who had been converted from Judaism—though his parents found it hard to understand that those who became Christians were not forsaking the privileges of belonging to the People of God, eventually to become the priests and servants of all men, but had found in Christ the means through which this could be fulfilled. At the same time there were not a few things in Christianity which alienated him. There was occasional baiting by Christian boys. There was a bigger gap between profession and practice in the two faiths, so it seemed, since all Gentiles he instinctively regarded as Christians. Even with professing Christians there were lower ethical standards (so it appeared), less warmth of heart and human understanding.

At Cambridge, where he was President of the Hebrew Congregation, he came into a life of intellectual freedom and stimulus to which both Jews and Christians contributed. Perhaps what appealed to him most forcefully was that his Christian friends witnessed by their lives rather than by their words. Unhappily he found dissension and a lack of community at the Jews' College.

After ten years he left the Jewish Ministry and joined the Civil Service but was still involved very fully in synagogue affairs, becoming a 'Ruler of the Synagogue' in Sheffield. To his dismay he found quarrels and enmity were all too frequent in the community. Slowly and unhappily he found himself following the outward form of his faith but steadily slipping away from its deeper beliefs and consolation. Like men of many faiths he moved into humanism, deeply committed to serving his fellows but utterly unsure of God.

A Christian colleague at work to whom he talked about personal worries asked if she might pray for him and he readily agreed, though it occurred to him (and somehow he found the thought comforting) that she was praying 'in the name of Jesus'. Then, one Sunday afternoon on Hampstead Heath in 1953, he set out to visit Keats' House, found it closed and walked a little way to Downshire Hill. He looked inside the Chapel of St John and there was introduced to the Minister.

Invited to lecture to the Fellowship there, he at first resisted the suggestion. 'I am a Jew,' he said.

The Minister looked at him. 'So am I,' said Dr Jakob Jocz, and invited him to tea. It was the beginning of a profound friendship. The pilgrim had found a guide who had himself passed the same way. Perhaps it was not surprising that a little later, in a Bloomsbury church, Eric Lipson left his own confession of Christ, verses written on a slip of paper, on the communion table.

There was nothing dramatic. No flashing light or heavenly voices on a Damascus road. Only a pilgrimage to a new certainty. Yet certainty there was, and a deep joy, so that Eric Lipson became the President of the International Hebrew-Christian Alliance and a worker for the Church's Ministry among the Jews.

NOBEL PRIZE-WINNER

Albert Luthuli, an African in his middle fifties, stepped off the plane in Johannesburg. A ban preventing him from visiting all larger African towns had just expired. He was met by two white policemen from the Special Branch. They asked his name, and presented him with two papers. There were two new 'bans', more strict than the earlier one, limiting his freedom of movement and association. Then, in case he did not understand, one of them barked out: 'Can you speak English?'

'A little,' replied the ex-chief, and smiled when the officer stumbled out a few words of Xhosa. His own language, in any case, was Zulu.

It was, to him, an illustration of the utter ignorance of so many white South Africans. For all his working life he had spoken English, at school and college and on the public platform. He wrote widely. His name was known throughout the country as well as far beyond it. But the Africaaner insisted that, like every other African, he was illiterate and a savage.

That such a man could maintain not only humility and a forgiving spirit, but his Christian faith in God and man, is a wonderful triumph of grace. A newspaper, reviewing his autobiography, spoke of him as 'one of the greatest men produced by Africa in this century . . . a far greater man than most of those who call themselves his masters.' That book is called *Let My People Go.* Albert Luthuli's whole life was given to the struggle, always peaceful and non-violent on his side, to achieve freedom, dignity and a full life for the African people.

He was born in Groutville, Natal, before the turn of the century, in a Congregational family, though he himself became a Methodist when he went to a Methodist boarding school. He took the obvious road of gifted young Africans and trained as a teacher. It was during this period that he lodged with a Methodist evangelist and his family. In this home he saw Christianity for what it really was and, though he would never date a moment of conversion or decision, it was there, and he put it, that his spirit was roused. The awareness of God's presence was with him ever afterwards.

There was plenty in the years that followed that would have made a lesser man lose faith.

At Adams College, to which he went with a bursary for further study, he stayed for fifteen years, mostly as a member of staff. There was a true community between Africans and whites, but Luthuli was all too aware of the indignities under which his own people lived. He could not follow the great Aggrey's advice, when he addressed the college, that 'half a loaf was better than no bread'. In striving for the whole much might be lost, but no true man could do less.

His first opportunity for service to his people came when he was elected by popular vote Chief of the Umvoti Mission Reserve, with his headquarters in his home town of Groutville. He accepted the duty reluctantly, not least because he knew he would be thrust into the forefront of the struggle for rights, and in particular for the right of Africans to own the land they tilled.

In 1938 he was appointed a delegate to the World Missionary Conference at Tambaram, Madras. The visit produced two conflicting memories. The first was that the African delegates were given second class passage and told by a Dutch Reformed minister not to join the white passengers in worship. The second was the vivid impression of equality and freedom enjoyed by Indians under the British *Raj*. At Tambaram there was a mixing of races, in debate, worship and eating, that exposed the *apartheid* of South Africa in all its shame.

For the following ten years his struggle was mostly within his own locality—opposition to the setting-up of a white-run beer-hall and to the erosion of native land for industrial purposes, a steady attempt to gain rights of land for the subsistence farmers of his Reserve. By 1948, however, 'rights' were already seen by white South Africans as 'privileges', and 'privileges' were being steadily withdrawn. That year Luthuli visited the United States, and felt something of the power of the growing civil rights movement. In the same year Malan became Prime Minister, and Dr Vervoerd Minister for Native Affairs.

Within a year the widespread fear and discontent had become formulated in the new African National Congress and by 1952 the Congress had initiated the 'Defiance Campaign'. Its purpose was, in Luthuli's phrase, 'to oppose a system, not a race' and, indeed, then and thereafter there were many whites who shared in the campaign and others that supported it. But *apartheid* (always only semi-visible to the tourist) was beginning to bite. Separate seating in public places, separate queues, in fact if not in theory separate churches and worship, separate toilets, separate standards of wages for the same kind of work, the refusal of the sort of education which would qualify blacks eventually to do jobs reserved for whites, 'the sort of condescension which made a white man speak of ''a good kaffir'' in the same way as he spoke of ''a good dog'' ' . . . and worse than all this the restrictions that made it impossible for a woman to move from village to town with her husband without danger of arrest, or a man to live with his wife who worked as a servant in a European household.

Luthuli was President of Congress, and he did not expect to escape the fury of the government. Official vengeance fell quickly, hard and often. In 1952 he was deposed as Chief. The Defiance Campaign brought bannings, banishments and arrests. Luthuli suffered a ban from all larger towns, and was banned again when he arrived at Johannesburg as soon as that one had expired. In 1955 he had a stroke, but went on with the preparations for the great 'Congress of the People' at Johannesburg.

Almost immediately after his Congress Luthuli was arrested for High Treason. Invoking its anti-Communist legislation the government pulled in people all over the country—blacks, whites, and Indians. At one point in this period twenty thousand people were under arrest, though only a small number were finally brought to trial. Some of those still in confinement include the finest Africans in the Union.

So the years went by, with pressure always increasing. The Pass Laws were tightened up—without a pass an African could not work, walk the street, remain in the town, live in his village or go from one to the other. For Luthuli there were more bans—'no meetings at all, and that means you and one other'. Talking to a group of Europeans by invitation he was beaten up and the chairman, a woman, flung from the platform. In 1960 came the Sharpville massacre, followed by the banning of the National Congress. In despair, Luthuli led the nation—as Ghandi had done in South Africa half a century earlier—by burning his pass in public.

What does this sort of life do to a man? To his faith?

Take just one comment. 'My cell became a sanctuary . . . the opportunity to rededicate myself . . . to be quiet in His presence.' His words and his writings show anguish but no bitterness, an incredulity that men should treat each other as they do but, deep down, an unshakeable faith both in man and God.

In 1961 he was awarded the Nobel Peace Prize, though he was not allowed to leave his own restricted area to go and receive it. But, to Albert Luthuli, the awareness of God's presence and approval in his struggle for his people's rights was of infinitely more importance than any other award he might receive.

ON TARGET

Much of Africa—East, West and Central—consists of countries which have moved from a colonial past into an independent present in less than a generation. That transformation has been accompanied by a maturity which would have seemed impossible to those earlier settlers who regarded rural Africa as too conservative to welcome change, backward if not positively barbarous.

The metamorphosis is exemplified most clearly in the lives of individuals, not in the complex changes of social or political life. Village farmers have become government ministers, primary school teachers have proved themselves distinguished heads of states, cattle-boys have turned into men of influence in many walks of life.

One of the young herdsmen who proved his ability and maturity was Henry Okullu, Provost of All Saints' Cathedral in Nairobi, the capital of Kenya.

Born in 1929 at Asembo Location in Central Nyanza, life held no more for his family than simple farming. He himself, with no hope of any more education than any other village child in the bush, was a herd boy caring for the cows and goats. Then, suddenly, he ran away. What no one would give him he would gain for himself. True he did not run far; only to a mission school a few miles from home. But his resolution and his bright face won him a place. He passed from primary to secondary school at a period when education was beginning to matter in East Africa, and when Church schools were providing vision and opportunity for a generation which was going to take over the running of their own countries more swiftly than anyone realised.

Church school it may have been at Kima, with prayers, Bible reading and scripture lessons, but none of it seemed to have any deep effect on young Okullu. He did not resent or resist the Church but he had little connection with it. From his first job at the Military Construction Unit in Mombasa he went on to join the East African Railway and Harbour Board, and it was only when his prospects were beginning to shine brightly ahead that he realised he must begin all over again. God was calling him into the Church. Against family opposition and the scorn of his friends he began to train as a priest at Bishop Tucker College in Uganda. In 1958 he was ordained and appointed to his first parish at Kakira.

Then, as so often happens, there came another twist in his life. He could never have been really satisfied with commerce. He might have been a writer, politician or preacher, but he would have to deal with words. Not only words, but words and people. Using words to change situations, to persuade people to think and act, to challenge complacency, conservatism and cant. He wrote a letter about 'the death of Lumumba', the Congolese leader, to the Christian newspaper *New Day*. It proved a new beginning. The editor quickly saw in this first letter the evidence of a wide-open and balanced mind.

In 1962 the young priest became assistant editor of *New Day*.

The old age, in which Christian communication was limited to the pulpit or preaching in the open air, was passing quickly. Radio, soon to be followed by television, was providing fresh platforms for Christian witness. Of increasing importance, too, were the new Christian newspapers in Africa and Asia, not merely reporting the parochial affairs of the churches but offering in their columns a place for fearless comment on every issue of the day. To use such an opportunity fully was to become involved in a dangerous trade. The Church is tolerated readily enough when it sticks to the affairs of the parish pump. It asks for trouble when it dares to pronounce on social, national and political issues.

Okullu's service with *New Day* did not last long. He went to America to study for a B.D. at Virginia Theological Seminary. But he did not get there as fast as he might have done. Instead, he stopped in England and worked for several months on the *Liverpool Daily Post and Echo* to learn more about contemporary journalism. The editor-in-chief was so impressed with the temporary recruit that he took him home to dinner, and then wrote to *New Day* to say that Mr Okullu's journalistic ability was outstanding.

Back in East Africa *New Day* died, and was succeeded by *Target*—in English, with its African-language edition, *Lengo*. Henry Okullu became the editor of *Target* at a moment when its future was uncertain because of its uncompromising Christian attitude to national policy and Government actions. Not only did he survive the storm without bending to it; he took the paper to a position of high influence throughout East Africa. 'Conscientious . . . courageous . . . balanced . . . sensitive'. Such were the words which described him in the issue of the paper which announced his appointment as Provost of the Cathedral.

His own phrase was: 'I believe God has a concern with everything that concerns his people.'

THE END OF DEVIL'S ISLAND

Young Charles Péan had no doubt about his future. He had begun training as an agriculturalist in order to become a colonial farmer in Algeria. He would follow in his uncle's footsteps. It was all quite clear—until he served for three weeks as volunteer chauffeur. That changed everything.

Péan *père* was a devout Roman Catholic banker, and Charles went in procession with the other choir boys at the age of four. When M. Péan died, still a youngish man, there came a dramatic alteration in Charles's life. His mother, a Protestant, began to bring up the family in her own faith, and emigrated to Algeria with her seven children to live with their uncle. It was an exciting life against a prosperous farming background. Plantations of olives, cereals, oranges and tobacco . . . herds of cattle, horses and sheep . . . a satisfying existence in the open-air, seemingly leading to fortune. For young Charles farming became the only thing imaginable. From school in Algeria he went to an Agricultural College in France.

At the age of eighteen he decided to have a holiday in Switzerland, but the frontier post pointed out that his passport was not in order. It contained an amateur photograph which must be replaced by a proper one. It might take a day or so to arrange. The passport officer suggested that there might be accommodation at a Salvation Army hostel in the little town of Audincourt nearby. There he found a bed and a temporary job. He was asked if he could drive and, since he had just taken out a driving licence, readily agreed to act as chauffeur to the Territorial Commander who was to conduct a mission in the area.

On the last day of the mission he was the first 'volunteer' to go to the penitent form.

A few days later, his holiday cancelled, he arrived at the Army's training college in Paris and asked to be accepted as an officer in training. To the officer in charge it was an absurd situation. No one could be accepted without at least a year in 'the ranks'—until the Territorial Commander whom Charles had driven round put in a special plea for him. To Charles it was almost equally absurd. He had no overwhelming sense of sin. He had not been 'converted'. He had simply seen that he must do something quite different with his life from anything that he had planned. Farming was finished—and he regretted it bitterly—but this was apparently what God wanted. He could have no idea that farming was, in fact, to be one of the skills which would make his real task possible.

In 1920 he was posted as a lieutenant to the Paris Central Hall, which was followed by national service and a number of other appointments.

Then, in 1928, came the decisive interview with the Commissioner. He was sent to conduct a tour of investigation of the French penal settlement in French Guyana—the terrible Devil's Island, one of the most notorious convict 'prisons' in the world.

Hard-core criminals did not 'sweat it out' in French gaols. They were shipped across to South America to live in conditions of the utmost foulness and horror. Even when they had served their sentence they were not free for the terrible *doublage* system then took over. The *libérés* must serve as long again in the islands as their original term before they might eventually be allowed to return to France. In the event, because they could neither save enough money for their passage nor avoid the temptations and violence of the islands, they rotted and died where they were, in the tropical heat with its constant sickness and debilitating moral climate.

All this Péan quickly saw for himself on that brief visit. His temporary houseboy had been transported for poisoning a whole family. The two men who pushed his 'car' on the track through the jungle were a murderer and a violent felon. In the terrible Islands of Salvation Péan found that a doctor had just been murdered and the whole population was in a state of riot and fear. Everywhere the *libérés* were drunken, tempted to escape into the forests where they died of disease, or ill with venereal disease which produced insanity. Some contracted leprosy. In the convict blocks, locked from sunset to dawn, the warders might easily find a man with his throat cut in the morning, but did little to find the culprits. They themselves might be killed if they did. When Péan fell ill with malaria a convict male-nurse sold the quinine and injected unsterilised water, producing ulcerations from which he suffered throughout his life.

Charles Péan returned to France with four main resolves. He would make France aware of the horrors of her penal settlements; he would gain permission for the Salvation Army to work there; he would strive for the return of the *libérés* at the state's expense; and, in the long term, he would struggle for the abolition of the whole evil system.

It was five years before he took his first tiny group of volunteer Salvation Army officers to Guyana but in that time he had shocked France by his book *Convict Country*. On his return to France he underlined the message of the first book with a second, *The Salvation of the Outcast*. Now, however, he had positive things to say. He had proved that salvation was possible. Not only had the officers begun hostels for the *libérés*, with carpenter's shops to make the furniture, but

Péan's agricultural training had been called into service. Montjoly Farm, with plantations of bananas, lemons, coconuts and pineapples stretching for miles had been begun. Men had real work, the beginnings of a home, and something to live for. The French conscience was touched at last and the first *libérés* began to return. Sixty-seven men were repatriated in February, 1936, and a boatload came every month that year. Péan himself was appointed to a national committee on penal reform.

In 1937 a bill was introduced into the Chamber of Deputies to end the scandal of the penal settlements. In 1938 it became law: the end was in sight.

It was to be a longer business than Péan and the Salvation Army had hoped because war broke out in 1939. France was occupied by the Nazis and the country torn between collaboration and resistance. The Salvation Army was banned on the absurd ground that it was an agent of the British Secret Service. Péan himself took up work with abandoned and delinquent children. Not until the war was over did he fly back to Devil's Island to find his old Army colleagues still at their posts, unrelieved for eight years, heroic but emaciated and stricken in health.

With Péan's arrival new hope swept the island, and this time it was not to be deferred. France began to make reparation for her years of guilty neglect. Slowly the repatriation scheme got under way, first to North Africa and then to France itself. Amongst those who came back were many who had already begun a new life, through the power of God made real in the work and witness of the courageous Army officers.

Charles Pean was given new responsibilities, as Commissioner of all Salvation Army work in France and Switzerland. He was made an Officer of the Legion of Honour. He became a permanent member of government commissions on penal reform.

But probably the most memorable day in his life was in 1952 when the Salvation Army furled their flag on Devil's Island to return home. The convict settlement was abolished. Devil's Island was ended and Charles Péan's great mission was accomplished.

THE ROOFS OF PARIS

The Second World War had been over for nearly ten years. The boulevards of Paris were bright again, even if the gaiety was a trifle brittle. Tourists made their way to the art collections of the Louvre and the nightclubs of Montmartre. On the pavements the street-singers struck the same sharp pre-war notes as they used to do, against the strident background of piano-accordions—old songs, shallow songs, cynical songs.

Sous les toits de Paris set bodies swaying and made the war and the winter seem a long way off.

But for all too many there were no roofs at all in Paris. 1953-4 was the bitterest winter France had known for two generations. Thousands of families were homeless and many were starving. A great city is no place to go hungry, for passers-by only look the other way when they see the ragged bundles on the park benches, under the dripping trees or in the gutters.

The people of Paris were suddenly shocked out of their apathy. An almost unknown priest broadcast an invitation to the Minister of Reconstruction to attend the funeral of a three months' old baby found in a disused bus.

The Abbé Pierre had fired the first salvo in a new war—a war on poverty, homelessness and degradation.

Henri Grouès was the fifth child of a wealthy silk merchant of Lyons, born in 1912. Luxury and indulgence came easily to him, and he seemed to be destined for the careless life of the rich. Then, just about at the time of his eighteenth birthday, his family had their first glimpse of what he was like, under the superficiality of his social life. He asked his father for his own share of the patrimony. 'Give me my own portion' may have reminded Grouès *père* of the prodigal son, but Henri's next action dispelled any fears the family might have had of his squandering his wealth in a far country. Squander it he did—but immediately, and where he was. Within twenty-four hours he had given it all away to the poor and, almost immediately afterwards, entered a Capuchin monastery under vows of perpetual obedience and poverty.

Eight years later the rigours of monastic life had proved too much for him. He left the monastery with tuberculosis and took up work as a priest in a village near Grenoble.

A monastic life was, in any case, unsuited to his active, vigorous temperament. That was quickly proved when war broke out. Within a year or so he had joined the French Resistance. Concerned to disrupt the Nazi rule in France, he refused to engage in violence but helped prisoners and refugees to cross the frontier. One, who collapsed, so that the priest had to carry him on his back to safety, proved to be a brother of General de Gaulle. He shared in forging documents and passports, joined in raids on German and Italian headquarters and began an 'underground' newspaper. It was during this period that he adopted the name of 'l'Abbé Pierre'.

By the end of the war he had been awarded six decorations, including the coveted Croix de Guerre and the Legion of Honour. After what he had been through the ordinary parish priesthood had insufficient appeal. He was a devout Christian, but for him Christianity implied action. In 1945 he was elected a member of the new parliament and again, in 1946, he was a Deputy in the Assembly. His home was a large, broken-down house in the Paris suburbs.

Such a house was too big for one man—far too big for a priest with a large heart. His first 'guests' were a young, unmarried Communist couple with a small child. He began transforming the house into a youth hostel—but the old needed helping, too. The house became a refuge for the down-and-outs. With the help of those who had flocked to him for help for themselves he built outhouses in the garden with such bits of wood as he could gather. All his salary as a Deputy went towards his work. His vow of poverty was one he never broke, and his vow of obedience was to Christ Himself.

Soon the ragged community had a name—the 'Companions of Emmaus'—which reminded all who came (and few had any religious associations) that Christ had walked with the sorrowful and shared their home and their bread.

It was an old rag-picker who suggested that the dustbins of Paris might hold bits of junk and rags which could be sold to provide funds for the 'House of Emmaus' and its charity. Soon the scavenging scheme grew too big for poor ragged men with sacks on their backs. L'Abbé Pierre needed a truck. In order to raise money for it he went on a radio quiz programme. His well-stored mind found the right answers so readily that he quickly won prizes amounting to 260,000 francs—enough for his first truck.

There were more scavengers, more trucks, more money, with the Abbé himself always involved in collecting, sorting and selling. Well-wishers added their own donations. All over Paris, in disused railway carriages, huts, empty houses, anywhere where there was shelter, l'Abbé Pierre made room for the poor who came to him in scores. 'Food and shelter for all the hungry and homeless who come,' was his motto.

At the same time he was using his position as a Deputy in the Assembly to pressurise the government into dealing with the problems of post-war Paris. His campaign reached its most vigorous point in that dreadful winter of 1953-4. It was then that he publicly asked the Minister in charge of reconstruction and rebuilding in Paris to attend the funeral of the dead, deserted baby.

Not only did the Minister attend the funeral. Much of the shocked citizenry of Paris seemed to go, too. It did not end there. France had been forced to face the reality of poverty. People were engaged in a new war, where victory could be seen only in terms of human dignity and opportunity. Immediately the Government decided to allocate a $2,540,000 for emergency housing. Ordinary people made an astonishing response. More than two thousand tons of goods almost submerged the Abbe and his Emmaus companions. Better still, within six weeks of his broadcast he received $1,016,000 in cash.

Within a year of his appeal the Companions of Emmaus occupied three shanty-towns—'villages' was too dignified a name for them—on the outskirts of Paris.

Hope was born again in the hearts of thousands because this tubercular priest, who had begun his own pilgrimage by giving away to the poor all that he had, lived out the compassion of the Lord he served.

THE LION'S SKIN

It is not given to many honest men to become the 'chief of the Criminal Tribes'. Or to many a railway-clerk to be offered 'the lion's skin', as the Rajputana people of western India called the traditional throne of the ruler.

But it happened to Samuel Rahator, the Methodist minister who made three separate lives for himself, one after the other, and did the work of a lifetime in all three.

He belonged to the hill-country near Nasik, and went to work as a clerk in the railway-sheds there. Befriended by a British engine-driver, and converted by a British soldier who preached in the sheds, he felt the call of the city—though hardly of the city lights. It seemed that God was calling him to the Bombay slums, and there he spent twenty long years. At first he had to teach English to clerks like himself to earn a few rupees, preaching at the cross-ways of the slum lanes in his spare time. When he was accepted as an evangelist, paid by the church, and later became a minister, it made little difference to his life. His manse remained in the *chawls*, as the Indian slums were known. He was called out to visit the dying, to mediate between quarrelling Hindu and Muslim neighbours, or try and quell the inter-faith riots that broke out all too frequently.

One day he walked into the British minister's house with a small, thin, wailing boy under each arm.

'A present for you,' he said. 'I've just picked them up outside your house.'

It was not surprising, for the worst famine in a century was sweeping across India. A visitor from Britain offered to pay for the boys' keep as long as it was necessary— and the Parel Orphanage had begun. His care for the children, his refusal to turn anyone away from his door, his love in action and his translation of the Gospel into practical terms made him one of the most respected Indians in Bombay. His future was clear. The slums had claimed him.

It was then that he had his dream.

He seemed to be standing in the jungle, hemmed in by dark trees. He saw a man on the path ahead of him lighting a small lamp and then walking on into darkness. The path led to a village. In his dream he saw that beyond the huts another lamp was lighted and beyond that was another village. There were more lamps—and more villages. Waking, he realised that the pattern of his life had been changed. God was calling him to leave Bombay, where he had spent twenty years in the streets, the mills, the factories, the orphanage and the church, to take light into the dark villages of the jungle.

He knew what these villages were like, for he had wandered amongst them as a boy when he trekked far out into the hills. At the entrance to each would be a Hindu temple, with a group of beggars and some uneducated priests in the courtyard. Every village would be in two parts—stone housing for the caste people, squalor for the outcastes. In many ways they were worse than the slums.

Three weeks later, with three evangelists to help him, he travelled up to Igatpuri, in whose railway-sheds he had been converted, and then out into the jungle. The preaching-tour began—and continued with little success. Where the field-workers wanted to listen the priests drove him out with curses, but for the most part there was little but indifference. Then, slowly, things changed. A farmer, who had once worked in the engine-sheds and had known the engine-driver who led Rahator to his conversion, offered him the use of a hut for a school. His talks, beginning with the simple things the farmers understood—the birds, the corn, the son who left home for the big town—fascinated the listeners. In Asvali, with the farmer's hut for school and church and already a few people baptised, he left one of his evangelists and moved on along the jungle trail. Ghoti, Akola, Sangamner, Rajur—the names of the villages along the jungle road were always in his prayers. In some places converts came quickly; in others there were none for seven or eight years.

In Sangamner the break-through came only when plague swept through the village and Rahator, arriving quickly with his little medicine-chest, picked up plague victims from the street and cared for them, while priests and people made their unavailing offerings to Mariamma, the smallpox goddess. In Akola it was almost as long. Then, after a few simple people had been baptised, there was persecution. It ended dramatically on a day when, throughout Britain, his fellow-Methodists were praying for this very man and this very village.

When at last the Marathi Mission was established and he imagined he would be based in the hills for the rest of his life, there came a final dramatic change. It arrived as a summons in a red-sealed official envelope—to go to see a distinguished Government officer in Bombay. The subject of their conversation was the Criminal Tribes. Rahator knew enough about them to make it a lively conversation. Once or twice he had been ambushed and nearly murdered by them. Living in hide-outs in the jungle, these men and women were shrewd, swift, unscrupulous and dangerous—criminals by caste and by the traditions of their tribes for centuries. But the sixty-year-old evangelist was not prepared for what followed.

'We want to turn these people into decent citizens . . . to resettle them here in Bombay . . . to get them working, and their children educated. You are the only man we can think of who might achieve it.'

Samuel Rahator knew it was too great a task, even for one who knew the jungle and its people as well as he did. But not too big for God, surely? Before many months had passed, in their secret hiding-place in the depths of the jungle, the Criminal Tribes made him their chief. Little by little the old ways were given up, few by few they came to a new life and a new faith. But not until the day when they set him on the stool covered with the 'lion's skin' could he really believe that he had the hearts of these men and women from the underworld of India.

One by one they touched the ground before him in deep respect.

'Where you go we will go,' said these proud and lawless men; 'what you tell us we will do. Your word is our law.'

WITH GOD IN FLEET STREET

Hugh Redwood's most famous book was written when he was past forty, and it was his first.

In January, 1928, the Thames burst its banks at Westminster, and tragedy swept through the basements of the slum houses. Ten people were said to have died that night, choked to death by the mud in the thick, filthy water. By 4.30 a.m. on 7th January the *News-Chronicle* was on the streets with a scoop story when comparatively few homes had radio-sets. The next morning Hugh Redwood, night editor of the *News-Chronicle*, was on his way home to Kent when something seemed to block his path. It was nothing physical, but an insistent feeling that he should go down to the flooded slums and offer to help. He got off the train, and turned back. He found that the people most busily at work were the Salvation Army Slum Post. The officers did not ask his name or where he came from; they just gave him a sack of old clothes to carry into the next street.

That day's story makes the first chapter of his first book. Redwood discussed it with the Religious Editor of Hodder and Stoughton, the publishers, taking the chapter for him to read. Arthur Hird had mentioned an edition of twenty thousand copies—'a bit high for a religious book'. When he had finished reading the chapter he changed his mind. 'We'll sell a quarter of a million!'

That book was *God in the Slums.* It was translated into sixteen languages and lifted Hugh Redwood immediately into the top flight of religious best-sellers. It did little to change the outward form of his life, however. He remained a working journalist, the career in which he followed his father's footsteps. His biography he called *Bristol Fashion*, but he might well have named it *God in Fleet Street.* It was there that he showed men how to walk with God.

The night of the floods was not Redwood's first encounter with the Salvation Army.

As a young Bristol reporter on the *Western Daily Press* he was sent to Broadmead Chapel to report Mrs Bramwell Booth, the daughter of the Army's founder. Coming from a middle-class home, where church-going was a somewhat meaningless Sunday occupation, he did not expect to be impressed. To his surprise he was deeply moved and, the next night, went to the Salvation Army Citadel. That evening he knelt at the penitent form. The inward result was peace and joy; the outward one, anger and hostility. His mother had hysterics; his father called him a fool and turned him out of the house.

He exulted in his 'persecution' and was quickly pressed into speaking about it in citadel meetings and in the open-air. For a while he was the show-piece of the corps which he joined as a 'soldier'. Though his conversion was real enough, he suffered from over-much publicity, too little training and only a rudimentary understanding of prayer. When a new officer took the place of the ensign under whom he had been converted and took the measure of the swollen-headed teenager, he brought him under discipline. There would be no more speaking, at any rate for some time.

How long the order was to be enforced Redwood did not wait to find out. Angrily he left the Army and his mother, with considerable pleasure, gave his 'blood and fire' uniform away.

Nearly a quarter of a century later he was trying to pick up a musical programme on the radio when he found himself tuned in to one of the most famous Sunday night voices of the time. Canon W. H. Elliott was talking about prayer. For the second time in his life Hugh Redwood was arrested, unable to escape the sound of the gospel. He went upstairs, knelt by his bedside and, in his own phrase, 'took the hand that God offered him'.

Life had begun again. To everyone he met in the next few weeks—and he was one of the most popular journalists in Fleet Street—it was evident that he was a changed man.

Prayer became the compelling power in his life.

Soon after his conversion his daughter Gwen, just about to leave school with every hope of a distinguished future, was stricken with polio. The doctor gave her seventy-two hours to live. Redwood had no other resource but prayer. When he came downstairs again he told his wife that Gwen would recover. He had had an assurance on this point that he could not disregard. He did not claim it to be an answer to his own prayers or his own faith; he saw it only as a certainty made known while he prayed. In the end Gwen did not die, though she spent many months in hospital. It was after leaving the hospital, where he had been visiting her, that he felt the compulsion to go back to Westminster and try to help the flooded slum-dwellers.

God in the Slums was written because Redwood was so impressed with the work of the Salvation Army that he offered to write a booklet about it to be sold at some of their sales of work. The booklet turned into a book, and the book into a best-seller, from which all the royalties went to the support of the Army's social service in the slums. Two years later came *God in the Shadows*, telling part of the story of his own pilgrimage. In 1934 he published *Kingdom Come*, a phrase-by-phrase exposition of the Lord's Prayer and, ten years after his conversion, *Practical Prayer.*

Fortunately he served a newspaper which not only had a great tradition but also an editor of high integrity and journalistic flair. Tom Clarke one day came into Redwood's room and said he thought it would be a good idea to print each day at the foot of the leader column one single sentence which would be crisp, uplifting and thoroughly Christian. Would Redwood try his hand? The result was *Today's Parable*, which ran for eight years. 'Dead pasts are best buried without post-mortems'. 'When tackling a hard nut, aim at cracking the shell without crushing the kernel'. These were typical of hundreds of original, apt, pithy comments. It was to *Today's Parable* that many readers turned first of all.

On the Saturday page appeared another Redwood item—a 'Lay Sermon'. They were first-rate journalism—readable comments on everyday practical religion. But they were neither shallow nor trite. They carried the marks of deep personal faith as well as a practised hand. Much of their significance for weekend readers who never went to church was that they were not written by a parson, but by a working-man like themselves.

The fact that Hugh Redwood was a layman gave him much of his influence. A bishop offered him ordination when he retired from the newspaper world, but Redwood rightly refused. It would have stifled him. Just as bad, it would have limited him within the confines of one denomination. Instead, he travelled widely, preached in cathedrals, chapels and citadels, and broadcast frequently. Over and over again he came back to the subject of prayer, the life-blood and the life-line of the Christian. It was not something he merely talked about. It was something he practised every day.

His was the only newspaperman's desk in Fleet Street which had on it a card-index in which were filed—for use—the names of those who wrote to him with requests for prayer.

MILLIONAIRE—AND MORE!

The cynics always assume that when a wealthy man gives money away he is trying to buy his place in the Kingdom of Heaven. When one of the richest men in the world announced that he was retiring from business specifically so that he could spend the rest of his life giving money away the cynics were not merely incredulous. They sought, and invented, reasons for his extravagant use of 'conscience-money'.

It was in 1910 that the world's newspapers carried the news of John D. Rockefeller's retirement. There were snide references to the way in which his father's wealth had been made and of how John had added to it. His private life was written up as though his natural austerity hid unimaginable evil. There was little attempt to hide the opinion that a man who retired to give away money was either crooked or a crank. Only here and there was any credence given to the true reason. Yet that reason was simple enough.

He believed that with power went responsibility, especially the power that money conveyed. That money was a gift of God, but only a gift held in trust. That money and influence must be used for the benefit of others, not least those who had not achieved the common rights of man.

Brought up in a fabulously wealthy home, the Rockefeller children were required to keep an account of how they used their pocket-money. As a child John gave himself to God. He signed a pledge of abstinence from alcohol and smoking. But, from the beginning, the Christian life was not for him a negative thing. It was completely positive. It consisted far more in 'giving' than in 'giving up'. That was why the most important account in his private schoolboy ledger was lettered 'A', and consisted of the money he tithed for God's specific purposes.

If wealth isolated him from many of his fellow-students at Brown University, his use of it isolated him even more from his rich contemporaries. Why did he not join in the drinking-parties? Why should he account for every penny, washing and mending his own clothes to save still more money? How could a man with so much opportunity for self-indulgence and self-gratification spend time in regular church attendance and teach a Bible-class at the local Baptist church? By some he was respected, but he had few intimates.

Back in the family business he learned the hard way. In his early ventures there were failures as well as successes, and his first deal cost him a million dollars. But the great business complex was built for advance and, with the innate financial genius of this shy, apparently cold man to direct it, money accumulated at an almost unbelievable rate. His 'Ledger A' account offered immense scope for good. He refused to make quick judgments on the way it should be used. His conclusion, after a great deal of prayerful deliberation, was that it must be spent on long-term projects of lasting benefit rather than merely 'given away', though spontaneous charity was by no means excluded.

His first great contribution came from the realisation that, throughout the world, diseases like malaria, hookworm, leprosy and others hardly then named, took a terrible toll. Within a short time he had given sixty million dollars to the setting up of the Rockefeller Institute of Medical Research—a munificent project which did much to change medical history.

To conquer disease was only one step in offering life to the developing world, however, and he had already seen that education was a major need. He gave a hundred and thirty million dollars for world education within a few years. On the basis of this concern with primary education was built up a great complex of involvement with higher education. Medical research and advance in Africa and Asia has been matched by support of the Theological Education Fund, which makes training possible for countless students and pastors all over the world.

He did not demand or expect thanks. He merely shrugged his shoulders, for instance, when he was turned back, as a late-arriving tourist, at the ticket-office of the palace of Versailles, to whose reconditioning he had given some two million dollars. But he reacted more sharply to vicious slander in the press, properly insisting that Christian stewardship should not be misrepresented as a personal bid for fame or new power.

He was a man of faith. He believed in his own country and its destiny. That was why he built the great commercial and cultural Rockefeller Centre in New York at a cost of a hundred and twenty-five million dollars in the days of America's greatest depression in the 1930's. It provided work and openly pledged his faith in the American future.

He believed in man, and because of this his greatest benefactions were given for world health and world education, that men, however unprivileged, might take their rightful place in world society.

But, above all, he believed in God, who made man the steward of all His gifts. He was still prayerfully exercising that stewardship when he died in 1960, at the age of eighty.

HAPPY FAMILY

'What are you doing on New Year's Eve?'

'Nothing.'

'Then,' said Roy Rogers, 'why don't we get married?'

Get married they did in 1947, Dale Evans, with one grown-up son, to Roy Rogers with two motherless children. For both of them it was a new beginning, and for Dale in particular a break with a past that had had too many colourful as well as drab days. Neither Roy nor Dale, however, could have guessed anything of what that new beginning signified.

Dale Evans—the name was given to her by one of her early agents—was born Frances Octavia Smith in 1912 in Texas. She never completely got rid of the accentAn extrovert, but far more sensitive than anyone realised, she played for recognition as soon as she could walk, and worked for fame as soon as she had any ambitions at all. Fame, to Dale, meant radio, films, the stage. All she achieved in the beginning was notoriety, for at the age of sixteen she ran away to marry a teenager somewhat older than herself. In no time she was divorced, with a baby boy.

Tom was to be her problem as well as her joy in the years immediately ahead. She loved him but, more often than not, had to hide him. Theatrical agents, radio programmers and film producers did not want stars with sons. Not that Dale achieved very much stardom in the beginning. There was secretarial work, with some radio spots in Memphis, Tennessee, and an attempt to conquer Chicago which failed disastrously. She went back home to Texas with Tom, now growing up. Then came a second marriage. It was happier than the first, and lasted longer, but after a few years that failed, too, as both wife and husband made separate careers for themselves.

Dale seemed born to have dreams that did not come true.

By the time the second marriage ended, however, Dale was making a name for herself, though not the one she had longed for. She was in Hollywood, making films. Her personal tragedy included a factor more bitter to her than her broken marriages. She had Tom with her and for the sake of her career she had to pass him off as her younger brother instead of her son. Tom himself, a committed Christian, put up with the situation uneasily for his mother's sake. Dale, on her side, gave as much time to him as she could, resisting the temptations of the film-world. She was clean-living, hard-working and, to some extent, successful. But the pictures she made were 'westerns'—a far cry from the glamourous musical comedy stage of New York she had once planned to conquer.

The real star of her pictures, however, was Roy Rogers—though for small fans the glory was stolen by Trigger, the Wonder-horse. Rogers was happily married, but tragedy struck when his wife Arlene died in childbirth, leaving Linda Lou and an adopted Indian girl, Cheryl, for him to care for. Marriage to Dale, a close friend, came naturally and happily.

Up to this point Dale would have claimed to be a Christian. She had lived decently, had a staunch code of behaviour and some form of belief. However she suddenly saw all this to be merely conventional, when Tom asked her to go to church with him and the minister preached about 'the house built on the rock'—with a special reference to family life. Dale was badly shaken and the next Sunday walked down the aisle in commitment. Roy's response to her exuberant announcement was placid.

'Don't go overboard!'

Yet only a short while later Roy, going to church with the whole family, did the same thing.

It might seem that such a family, committed to Christ and turning to a new life, could have expected life to be all joy. It certainly seemed as if this new happiness would be crowned by the birth of their first baby, about which the whole family was throbbing with excitement. But Dale caught German measles during her pregnancy, and the little girl, Robin, was born a mongoloid child. Desperately grieved, Dale determined to bring her up as much a normal child as possible. Now, indeed, the family came first. But Dale, always frightened of death, had to face Robin's death when she was only two years old. It was during Robin's brief lifetime that Roy and Dale met Billy Graham, and were warmed by his understanding and his faith.

Already both Roy and Dale had begun to use their many public performances as occasions for Christian witness, and now a new note of compassion was linked with their proclamation of faith. If God could hold them during a period of such tragedy as they had passed through, then God was big enough for every situation. Not only a new confidence but new ways of witnessing came with Robin's death.

The first was Dale's desire to tell Robin's story—or, as it turned out, to 'let her tell it herself'. *Angel Unawares*, a book that swept America, was written as if this tiny child were indeed telling it herself. Its royalties brought new funds to the Association for Retarded Children: and its telling gave comfort to many in the same situation. It was the first of a number of high-selling books, for Dale suddenly found she could write as effectively as she could speak.

The other opportunity for Christian witness came with Billy Graham's invitation to join him in his campaign in Britain. Despite an initial hostility from the press, both to Dale and Roy as well as to the Graham team, the three 'westerners'—for Trigger was there, too—opened many hearts to the power of God.

There could be no more children born to Dale, but nevertheless the family grew. First, they decided to adopt a baby girl, a Choctaw Indian, from a children's home in Dallas; they walked out with a small boy as wellDodie and sandy were followed by a Scottish girl, whom they had met on their British tour and invited to visit them on their ranch. She, too, stayed. More and more the family—Roy's boy and girl now beginning to make their own lives—took an increasing part of Dale's time, though there was plenty left for family holidays, personal appearances and occasions for public witness. Radio, TV, press and magazines seldom left them alone for long. Ai Lee, soon to be called Debbie, had joined the family, too—a Korean orphan from the war-zone.

If there were anxieties they were those which come with every growing-up family, the sort of problems and joys which linked them with other American families. The Rogers' house was seen to be indeed built on the rock. It was that which gave credence to the things they wrote and said. To many it must have seemed that 'religion' itself offered a guarantee of security. That, at any rate, was shown to be far from the truth, Debbie, the charming Korean girl, now in her teens, was killed in a road accident. Not long afterwards Sandy, adopted after Robin's death, died suddenly in the army in Germany.

Love for the family leaves every member of it vulnerable. The deeper the love, the more anguished the wound when the circle is broken. Dale Evans Rogers was no exception. She was no stoic; the hurts went deep. Yet faith triumphed here, as always. The love that would not let them go offered power as well as peace, and joy remained.

ISLAND QUEEN

Two queens caught the imagination of the thronging crowds on the coronation route in 1953. One was Elizabeth II, just crowned in Westminster Abbey, young, happy, riding with all her newly-invested majesty in the golden state coach. The other was tall, big-boned, brown-skinned, exposed to the rain in her open landau, her gay smile and flashing teeth catching the eye even more effectively than her scarlet cloak. This was Queen Salote of Tonga. After their own queen, Londoners and provincials gave her their loudest cheers.

Yet, even when they saw her, many of them would have been unable to pick out Tonga, the only independent kingdom in the Pacific, amongst the myriad islands on a map of the South Seas.

There are two hundred islands in Tonga—the 'Friendly Islands'—and though most of them are small, between thirty and forty are inhabited. To one of them, Tongatapu, came Walter Lawry, the first Methodist missionary, in 1822, building a mission house which fell into decay when he left. He was the first of a series of missionaries to one or other of the main islands. There were three main territories within the group, ruled over by related kings, all descended—so the islanders believed—from the same king-god. One of the kings, Tubou, finally accepted the Christian faith in 1828.

It was in 1829 that king Taufa-ahua of Ha'apai came to Tubou's territory in his great canoes to plead for a missionary. None was available. Instead, he was offered the service of Peter Vi, a Tongan Christian teacher. It was only second-best in Taufa-ahua's eyes; indeed, it was little more than an insult when he wanted a white missionary. Furiously he set out to row back to his own island, only to find his fleet of canoes almost wrecked by a sudden storm. It seemed like a vengeance of the God whom he wanted to worship, and he turned back to accept Peter Vi as his instructor in Christian ways and faith.

On 7th August, 1831, Taufa-ahua was baptised and took the new name of King George. His children, too, were given Christian names, or in one case, at any rate, a western one. They were Tafita (David), Josaia and Salote (Charlotte) after the English queen.

The years that followed saw a slow but profound transformation in the islands. They had known war but not, as in many island-groups, cannibalism. Their problems arose from the scattered nature of the islands, the power of the pagan priests, the tensions between various tribal groups. King George's achievements, with John Thomas, the missionary son of a blacksmith, at his side, lay in the quiet reforms and justice he brought to the islands. These culminated after his visit to Sydney in 1853 in the creation of the Tonga Code, its laws based on Christian conceptions of human rights, liberty and justice. Tonga was, and is, a Christian country in more than name.

When her father died without any sons to carry on the line, Salote Tubou, great-grand-daughter of King George I, became Queen.

Educated at the Diocesan High School at Auckland, New Zealand, in an Anglican atmosphere of devotion and discipline, the young princess shared the lives of Maori girls who regarded themselves as her equals. If she was a little remote or austere, this tall young princess was so by temperament rather than from any sense of royal privilege. Back in Tonga, she married Prince Tungi when she was seventeen and in 1918 succeeded to the throne on her father's death.

She was a member of the Free Methodist Church (a Tongan variant of world Methodism) and the royal chapel was, in fact, the chapel of her people. The Tongans are a church-going People. Their lives and laws are based on a Christian respect for God, and for man as His creation. While they have the typical Pacific islanders' exuberance at festival times they are, for the most part, quiet, peaceful, truly 'Friendly Islanders'. By the queen's order, continuing that of her ancestors, there is almost complete prohibition of alcohol in the islands.

Kingship was tried in Hawaii, in Fiji and in Tahiti. It failed to endure in any of them. Only in Tonga has it lasted. That it has grown more, rather than less, secure with the passing years is due very largely to the moral stature and Christian grace of a queen who commanded the love as well as the loyalty of her people. She did so, in no small measure, because she shared with them the certainty and security of a profound, personal Christian faith.

THE OTHER SIDE OF THE BAY

One side of the Bay of Naples is well-known to the tourists who have Naples as a 'must' on their list of 'places to see in Europe'. The exquisite bay . . . Vesuvius in the background, with Pompeii below . . . Capri and Ischia . . . the waterfront, the cafes and the opera. The other side, for the most part, only Neapolitans themselves know—the torrid lanes and squalid alleys, the crowded tenements, the poverty.

It was in one of these narrow lanes that Teofilo Santi was born, and there that he grew up in Casa Materna, the Methodist Orphanage—not because he was an orphan but because the parsonage in which his father and mother lived had somehow, by chance or providence, become a haven for the unwanted children of the Naples slums. With his sister and two brothers he shared the security, the love and the privations of a home with twenty or thirty children—first in Naples itself, and from 1920, in the dilapidated princely villa at Portici, a few miles round the bay.

Children have always been part of Teofilo's life.

So was music, in the early days, for his mother was a musician of standing. His own choice of a career was not easy. Music, like his brother Emanuele, the violinist? The ministry, like his father? But in the end he decided on medicine. That was not easy, either, for there were no Protestant students at the medical school of Naples University and when he finally qualified he was to be known through Naples as 'the Protestant doctor'. That, in itself, meant suspicion, antagonism and even persecution from narrow-minded priests and superstitious slum-dwellers.

The Santis were used to difficulties. There was always lack of money for a family which by that time numbered nearly a hundred. There was constant harassing by the Fascist authorities, with attempts to close the school and orphanage, and his father was dragged off to the courts under suspicion of plotting against Mussolini's dictator-state. Yet long before the war broke out Teofilo had established a reputation for both skill and compassion and had helped to break down the barriers between Catholics and Protestants in the suburb of Portici, where he had established his surgery in Casa Materna itself.

During the war he was able to share the responsibility for the running of Casa Materna with his father and his lawyer brother Fabio, as well as maintaining his own medical practice, since he was an army doctor at the Port of Naples military hospital. Soon, however, there was more work than ever, for Naples became a major target for the allied bombers. Devastation swept through the city and nearly half its inhabitants sought refuge in the 'caves', the deep tunnels in the hills behind the city from which the stone for its building had been quarried through the centuries. Hating the Germans and their own Fascist government, the people of Naples prayed for peace.

The end came with Italy's capitulation in 1943.

By that time Teofilo had been moved to Capua, on the road to Rome, where he was medical officer at the prisoner-of-war camp. Like most of his colleagues he rejoiced at the news of the surrender. But their thanksgiving was all too brief. On the night of the capitulation American aircraft swept inland to bomb the road-bridge over the Arno at Capua in order to prevent the German troops round Naples escaping towards Rome. At dawn Teofilo clawed his way from the ruins of the medical mess, the only survivor in the house. Everywhere he was assailed with the screams of the wounded and the sight of the dead.

'I felt,' he wrote, 'as if I had had a resurrection. I not only had to offer thanks that I was saved. I had to ask *why* I had been saved.'

Though he was able to give help once more to the children of Casa Materna, who had been evacuated with his assistance to the lovely village of Positano, it was clear that greater tasks than this must lie ahead. As a doctor the agony of a blitzed and devastated Naples appalled him. Indeed, at first it paralysed him. There was so much to do that he was almost driven to do nothing.

One afternoon an American doctor, part of an investigating group visiting the city, took him to the 'caves'. He scrambled through the long, dark tunnels, stinking of dirt, excrement and hopelessness. Some of these refugees from terror had not seen daylight for months. He wanted to be sick, to forget the horror of it, to run away.

Instead, the next afternoon he brought a small table, his medical bag and what medicines he could gather together and started a daily clinic at the entrance to the caves. Then, with his brother Fabio, he began a campaign to persuade the Municipality, already hard-pressed with post-war problems, to have the refugees rehoused and rehabilitated. It was a long time before they were successful but, in time, and in makeshift quarters and barracks, new life came to the desperate people.

Long before that happened Teofilo had started another clinic in his father's old church near the city centre in Naples. The red crosses still remain on the windows. It was here that the first meetings of the Evangelical Hospital Committee took place. 'Why,' they asked, 'should not the Protestants themselves run a hospital for their own people?' 'And,' insisted Teofilo, 'for *any* of the poor, whatever their church.' Such a suggestion seemed almost a fantasy since the Evangelicals, for the most part, were drawn from the poorer sections of the community. Teofilo insisted that friends could be found to help—and went out to find them. As a result, there suddenly appeared the possibility of a hospital being built on the heights of Posillippo, overlooking the Bay.

The scheme came to nothing, the Municipality turning it down. A Protestant hospital in such a commanding position was unthinkable.

Teofilo wondered how he could ever have thought that he would have time to serve it, anyway. By this time he was committed to running a settlement, Casa Mia, in an old warehouse in the slums, in addition to all his other work, his private practice and the children of Casa Materna.

'We must have faith'—this is one of the reiterated phrases of the Italian Evangelicals. 'If God wants a thing done, He will see that it is done'—that was a Santi phrase, based on sixty years of experience that proved it true.

It appeared that God wanted another hospital in Naples.

The dream has become reality. The Communist-dominated, poverty-stricken suburb of Ponticelli, over-crowded with children and unemployed men, is almost devoid of welfare and education. The new Milan-Sicily *autostrada* runs by its side. There, between the town and the motorway, the Evangelical Hospital was opened in October, 1969. With a staff of Protestant and Catholic doctors and specialists, serving freely under a German matron and a group of international nurses, and with a staff of Protestant and Catholic doctors and specialists, serving with Teofilo Santi as the general superintendent, it builds new bridges between communities and offers new life.

THE LION OF JUDAH

In 1930, at the age of thirty-seven, Lij Tafari Makonnen became Emperor of Ethiopia. He took his baptismal names as his regal ones. Haile Selassie (it means 'Power of the Holy Trinity') had at last become the undisputed ruler of one of the oldest nations in the world, a country that claims to have the longest Christian history of all.

It was a long and dangerous struggle which brought him to the throne.

The royal succession in Abyssinia is not defined as in most nations. The Emperor nominates his own successor, though it is understood that he, or she, will be of the royal blood. The violent old Emperor, Menelik, had died without a son. His likeliest successor was Haile Selassie's father, but he died before the emperor and on Menelik's death there was a struggle for power that went on for twenty years.

Ethiopia—until it became one of the nations of the modern world it was known by its traditional name of Abyssinia—was a wild, lawless, violent land. There was only one road which partly linked the capital, Addis Ababa, to the coast. Travel was by unshod mule or donkey, and it might literally take months to reach the border from the capital. Slavery and slave-trading were basic to the country's life. Many of the people were Muslims, especially in the outlying regions. Prostitution was as widespread as slavery. There was practically no communication between Ethiopia and the outside world, and those foreigners who went to Addis Ababa found it without sanitation, electricity or amenities.

An immense amount remains to be done throughout the whole country. That Haile Selassie has achieved so much is tribute to his own vision, strength of character and absolute authority.

The new Emperor looked insignificant. A tiny man, with an olive complexion and a dark beard, always dressed in drab clothes, often with a cloak and a bowler hat, he seldom showed much animation. But his behaviour through the intrigues against his life before he finally reached the throne show a remarkable strength of character. He had not only a capacity for patience but, as many of his advisers felt, too great a capacity for forgiveness. Caught up in violent plots, he was the least violent of men. In a land where Christianity did not go very deep his own nature was Christian indeed. The Ethiopian dynasty proudly claims a direct line back to the Queen of Sheba, and the Church certainly derives from the earliest Christian centuries. Linked with the first

Christian community in Alexandria, it is part of the Coptic Church. Haile Selassie remains a devout member of that Church, with its primitive pageantry and its rock-hewn temples built to withstand early persecution.

In 1923, to the astonishment of the 'great nations', Abyssinia became a member of the League of Nations. The Christian heritage of other member states did not prevent one of them, Italy, invading Abyssinia in 1935, nor did it dissuade others, like Britain, France and America, from betraying the tiny League member by leaving it to its fate. Not until the weak, frightened pre-war governments were out of power did Britain come to her aid. Then at last, commanded by a young, Old Testament-type of army officer, Orde Wingate, columns marched against the Italians, drove them out of the mountains, and brought Haile Selassie back to his capital in 1941.

Coming to power in a mediaeval state in 1930, Haile Selassie needed at least ten years to bring his planned reforms into being. He had no time whatever, and had to begin all over again in the post-war years. There are many young Ethiopians who are depressed by the slowness of progress, and affected by left-wing policies after travelling in Europe. It is true that the rural areas remain much as they were. Even so, the contrast is remarkable. True, in the mid-1960's there were only 280,000 school places for a population of eighteen million—but when Haile Selassie went to school there were places for less than three hundred. There are only 5,700 beds for a population where smallpox, syphilis, hookworm and leprosy are endemic—but in 1940 there were no hospital beds at all. There are sixty Ethiopian doctors; twenty years ago there were none. Though roads in the rural area remain primitive, air communication links cover the country.

Addis Ababa is the headquarters of the Organisation of African States, and in choosing it the African leaders hailed the Emperor as the most significant statesman in the continent.

At the age of Seventy Haile Selassie was still working a twenty-hour day. For the rest, he regularly slept for three hours and prayed for one. To the Emperor it seems a fair division of time—and his hour of prayer remains today, as it has throughout his life, the source of his patience, his courage through all his personal tragedies, and his faith.

THE CRICKETER

Cricket, more than any other sport, has always been regarded as 'the parson's game'. On countless village greens and bumpy fields the vicar has turned out on Saturdays throughout this century. Not a few clergymen have played for their counties. But David Sheppard, striding to the M.C.C. dressing-room in his clerical collar, is in a class by himself.

He always loved the game, from the time he played it at his prep school and even before. At the age of seventeen he was chosen for the first eleven at his public school, Sherborne. An inauspicious beginning; he got a 'duck' in his first match, and again in his second. They were to prove far from typical entries in the score book.

Before long he was playing for his own county, Sussex, and making something of a name for himself as a batsman. Just as significant, he was liked for himself. Under the gentle courtesy a firmness of principle was clearly evident. Mostly his natural characteristics derived from his home background, developed by the self-awareness which is part of public school life. If religion played any part in his life, it was only that which was common to many Englishmen, a formal acknowledgment of a decent code of behaviour maintained rather than stimulated by attendance at the parish church.

In Belfast, during his early days of national service, he found a congenial atmosphere in the Sandes Soldiers' Home. After his period as an officer was ended, he went to Cambridge, where he found it easy to discuss religion with other undergraduates. But such debates were intellectual exercises rather than holding any personal reference to faith in Christ. In the same way, his early life in Sussex and his educational background gave him little concept of the pressures on people who must live their lives in the inner city or its east end.

Somewhere in his life there was a deficiency and he was vaguely aware of it.

The moment of change came when he attended a University Mission Service at Great St Mary's with another student, John Collins, and then returned to Collins' rooms for a discussion that went on into the small hours. The dramatic has little part in David Sheppard's temperament and there was nothing spectacular in what followed his intimate talk with Collins. He just went back to his own room and prayed to God.

'Come into my life,' he asked simply. 'I am willing to go with you . . . please keep me willing.'

It was not a shattering moment, a sudden reversal from sinfulness to godliness. Nevertheless, everything was changed.

One of the first questions he had to ask himself was whether it was right to spend so much time playing cricket. The answer seemed to be that it must depend on circumstances. No one suggested—not even his prayers prompted the thought—that he should exchange one kind of life for another. To 'go into the church', or give himself entirely to social welfare, or go out and preach on street corners were not courses that arose as realistic choices. In the event, cricket remained a way of life and a career.

Still playing for Sussex he found himself chosen for the 1950 Test team to tour Australia. In 1952 he captained the Cambridge University team and in the same year played the Test series against India. By 1953 he was captain of Sussex—and they came second in the county championship. Yet, within this agreeable pattern of life, a conviction was forming in his mind. He did not reach it as a result of any sort of anguished debate within himself. Rather, in his own explanation, it was an example of Isaiah's word about God: 'You shall hear my voice from *behind* you'—while you're getting on with the job.

He came to see that most of the things he wanted to do he would do better if he were ordained. Long conversations with Christian friends helped him. Prayer helped more. In 1955 he was ordained in St Paul's Cathedral and went as a curate to St Mary's, Islington. His wife, Grace Isaac, he had met at Cambridge.

It was not the end of cricket, however. Called to play in the fourth Test against Australia at Old Trafford in 1956, he scored 113 out of the 459 while Australia was all out for 84. There were Test matches against the West Indies, too.

Then, in 1960, came the painful question he had been wrestling with for some time—of playing against an all-white team labelled South Africa. He refused to play, and gave his reasons publicly. This was the first step towards an increasing involvement in the controversy about whether it was right to play cricket against a racially segregated team. In 1970 he became chairman of the Fair Cricket Campaign which played a considerable part, largely behind the scenes, in the calling off of a South African tour to England.

His work in Islington brought him to know by experience what it meant to live in the inner city. In 1958 he became Warden of the Mayflower Family Centre in Canning Town, by the docks of the East End of London. There was a whole complex of activities for all ages, with himself at the centre but delegating responsibilities in order to help others develop. It touched every part of the inner city community. There was, of course, a youth club, and a nursery school. There were groups for adults and clubs for the elderly. There was open house in his own home—and a special welcome into family life for those who found faith difficult and the Church largely irrelevant. If it was not in his nature, or his wife's, to bulldoze through other people's personalities and impose his own beliefs or standards, it was just for that reason that he made such an impact both on the simple and unsophisticated in his parish and on those with intellectual qualities and trained skills.

No people could have been happier than those of Canning Town when he was chosen again to play against Australia in the 1962 Test series. None were more certain of the good sense of the Church authorities when he was consecrated Bishop of Woolwich in 1969.

THE CIRCUS OF FATHER JESUS

It is not surprising that Father Jesus—a common name in Spain—is dedicated to the circus. It runs in his family's blood.

But he is even more dedicated to the clowns, the trapeze artists, the gymnastic cycle-riders, for all of them are boys—*his* boys.

La Ciudad de Los Muchados—the 'Boy's City'—is three miles from Orense, at Bompesta. The green countryside of Galicia, in the western corner of Spain, is a land far removed from the typical dry, brown, barren plains, or the sun-soaked congestion of the lidos and bays on the tourist routes. Here the village of Bompesta is the headquarters of a highly professional circus, the only circus training-school west of Budapest. Beyond the pine-covered slopes of the hills, to the astonishment of any visitor who penetrates this far, is a 'big top'. In this now bedraggled tent the boys of the circus toured Spain and began to make a name for themselves. Nowadays, instead, they play in the international circus centres—Geneva, Nice, Paris and London. In the tent swing the trapeze artistes; outside, tumblers fling themselves about; three or four boys do tricks on an ordinary bicycle; here and there, with bulbous noses and painted faces, the clowns work out their routines.

Everywhere, in the tent, the offices, the workshops, along the roads, moves the man in black . . . black corduroys, black sweater, black leather jacket, black curly hair . . . the short, stubby figure of Father Jesus Silva.

Though a grand-uncle had joined the Castilla family in founding the most famous circus in Spain, the Price Circus in Madrid, Jesus Silva belonged to a professional family of standing in Orense. His father was an architect and young Jesus intended to follow the same profession. Life was beginning to change when he grew up in Spain. He was born in Franco's own province, Galicia, the year before the General came to power in 1932. He was only a child when the Civil War ravaged Spain, and knew nothing of politics, Yet, as he grew through his teens, he became increasingly aware of the poverty of the Spanish people and, though he had not travelled beyond its borders, he was oppressed with the lack of freedom—freedom to think, to act, to make decisions.

Never a politician, never a rebel priest like some of the Basques from the north, his life has nevertheless been dedicated, in one of the most unlikely ways possible, to getting rid of poverty by producing a means of livelihood for hundreds of boys. At the same time, he has been building not a mere hope but the reality of democracy in his tiny city-state.

The wish to become an architect like his father died when he slowly became obsessed with the needs of the ragged waifs, the unwanted boys, the orphans of Orense's slums. Those in the best position for helping children were surely the priests, he thought. As a servant of God within the Church he could serve them himself, perhaps run an orphanage, certainly gain the support of the wealthy and professional laity as he could in no other way. He offered himself for the priesthood.

In 1957 he was ordained.

But, a year before that, his work had begun.

Riding a rackety motor-scooter he was already a familiar figure in Orense, often with a small boy clinging to the back. Amongst the children he was welcome wherever he went. By 1956 he had gathered fifteen boys, all unwanted or homeless, and lodged them in his mother's large house in the centre of Orense.

Then he remembered a film in which Spencer Tracy had starred. *Boy's Town*—the story of Father Flanagan of Chicago. Could he do something of the same sort? His mother and his brothers encouraged the idea. But, to his amazement, the Church authorities did not. The Bishop of Orense rebuked him, and thrust aside young Father Jesus's extravagant ideas. His job was to be an obedient parish priest.

When Father Jesus made it clear that, against all opposition, he was determined to serve the lost boys of Galicia, the bishop cut off his stipend. But by that time the twenty-five year old priest was committed to his own version of 'Boy's Town'.

His mother's house was overflowing with boys. The big rooms had been turned into dormitories, workshops, classrooms and a gymnasium. Within a year or so the news spread throughout Galicia. Boys arrived by themselves; boys were brought by a father or mother; boys cast-out, boys neglected, boys orphaned all found their way to Orense. Soon there was no more room. In the early 1960's, Jesus's lawyer-brother Jose bought thirty acres of pine-forest a few miles outside the city and presented it to Jesus and his boys.

'Bompesta', the new city-state, was created.

Now these wide acres hold a thousand boys of all ages up to sixteen or over. The centre of it all is the circus, the 'Circo de los Muchados'—and what *muchacho*—what boy—could resist its life? But there is much more than the circus involved in Bompesta. It is self-sufficient; it grows its own food and bakes its own bread; it has its own filling-stations and printing works, its own offices and its own bank. All are run by boys many of whom were illiterate when they arrived. Soon it may have its own hotel for tourists and visitors.

But it has a more important function than offering work, excitement, the chance to learn crafts and professional skills, with work in the morning and school each afternoon. It has its own government. In an almost entirely non-democratic country it holds its own elections, appoints its own mayor and council, runs its own affairs. These boys are learning the responsibilities of democracy. Though they will find it hard to practise them when they become part of Spanish adult life, their ideals will not fade.

Religious observance is a matter for private decision in Bompesta. But, in a land where the Church is increasingly suspect for its defence of an autocratic regime, many of the hundreds of boys who leave this Spanish Boys' Town will remember that their love for freedom and their first chance in life came from Father Jesus Silva, a man who loved boys because he loved God.

BORN TO PREACH

Oswald Smith always knew he would be a preacher. More than this, by the time he was twenty he was convinced that it would be his destiny to preach to crowds. He could never have been convinced that this was mere ambition. He believed it was the will of God.

He believed he had been born to be an evangelist.

Time has proved him right. In his long ministry he has undertaken nineteen world tours through seventy-two countries. Never as a sightseer, always proclaiming the Gospel, this tall, stringy man, every movement betraying an intense and barely controlled energy, has become familiar in six continents.

Tens of thousands of people have thanked God for his ministry, even though they heard him for only one night, for through that ministry they have entered into new freedom and life.

Born in Ontario in 1889, it was perhaps because he was a railwayman's son that his vision for himself and the future began so early. Through his father he was able to get a free pass to travel to Toronto, at the age of sixteen, to attend a mission in the Massey Hall conducted by the famous evangelistic team, Torrey and Alexander. He sat through eight mission services in this hall which was to become so familiar in his own ministry, and came forward in dedication without hesitation when the moment for decision came.

Now he wanted only to serve God. With little opportunity to use the talents he never doubted he possessed, he went to live in Toronto, working in one office job after another . . . and speaking wherever he could. He taught a class of girls in Sunday school. He spoke at Bible classes. He talked of things he knew nothing whatever about—like the religious state of Japan and its need for missionaries. But this was not enough. He wanted to give his whole time to service, not a part of it. Turned down by the Presbyterian Church as an evangelist—he was barely eighteen—he offered himself to the Bible Society of Canada and was sent to the Muskoka region of Ontario. There he sold more Bibles than anyone had sold before.

It was on that trip that he first had the chance to preach.

Asked by a Methodist minister if he would take services on the Sunday he agreed without hesitation—and without thinking it necessary to say that he had never preached before. In the morning he recited one of the best sermons he had heard. In the afternoon and evening he extemporised. In the little country chapel he imagined he saw thousands in front of him, instead of a tiny group of countrymen.

But it was to be a long time before the crowds were there in reality.

After a six-day journey across Canada, he sold Bibles and preached to the Indians of British Columbia, and then came back to Manitoba College to begin training for the ministry. He found it would take nine years before he would be fully qualified. Knowing his need of further education he nevertheless objected to the time it would take to achieve it and, because the college was unsuited to his evangelical temperament, he left and enrolled at the Toronto Bible College. Chosen to speak on one of the more select occasions he told his friends that he thought he had done 'pretty well'—and consoled himself with the reflection that if he did not turn out well enough to be an evangelist he could always be a missionary!

Then, talking with a visiting preacher, his brashness and callow ambition was suddenly exposed. 'If you want to be an evangelist, you can be one on the foreign field . . . but if your 'evangelism' is only based on the wish to speak to large crowds it doesn't amount to much!'

That night, December 8th, 1910, still only twenty-one, he wrote in his diary: 'The great struggle is over. I surrender completely to God.'

Tall, taut, intense, he burned with an inner passion. He was never to be without ambition, seldom without certainty. He would desert one church for another, one place for another, even though no apparent opportunity or appointment lay ahead, because he believed God beckoned him forward and away. The next twenty-five years was to be a period of movement, of constant new beginnings, not infrequently of poverty and sometimes of rejection. Not even marriage would allow him to put down roots in any one place.

There were brief pastorates in Presbyterian churches in Chicago and a desperate few months in the hills of Kentucky before be became assistant pastor to J.D. Morrow at Dale Presbyterian Church in Toronto in 1915. This he has always counted as his first settled ministry. When Morrow enlisted as a chaplain to accompany American troops to France, Smith remained as acting pastor. 'Keep Dale a ''People's Church'',' were Morrow's last words to him. It was a phrase which was to remain for ever in Oswald Smith's mind.

But Smith demanded a renewed church, too. He prayed for revival, and preached for it. At last it came, in 1917. But if it changed some it alienated others. A significant and powerful group of church members objected to his methods even more than his message. In the face of growing opposition he resigned in 1918.

There followed a period with the Shantymen's Association in Vancouver; another few months when he had no church at all; five years' ministry in Toronto, beginning in the YMCA auditorium and then in the Parkdale Tabernacle. Here his gifts for organisation and, in a true sense, showmanship, became manifest. He used visiting preachers, singers, groups, distinguished missioners to back up his own ministry—and began to display his talents for raising large sums of money, especially for missions. It was while he was here that he undertook his first foreign tour—a mission in Latvia, Lithuania, Poland and Western Europe. The response to his preaching and his appeals astonished him. On his return the crowds flocked, greater than ever, to hear the message of a 'world traveller'.

Restlessness and indecision swept over him again. California, Los Angeles and back to Toronto again—to the Massey Hall where he had been converted. Never really since his experience at Dale belonging to any denomination he now allied himself with the Worldwide Christian Couriers, moving from Massey Hall to St James Presbyterian church and then, finally, in 1934 to Bloor Street, to an empty Methodist church. He gave it a new name.

It became 'The People's Church'.

And so it has remained.

One of the world's leading evangelists, Oswald Smith dedicated himself—swinging full circle from his early values—to the support of world mission. Missionaries became his chief concern. At Massey Hall his congregation supported forty missionaries in the Baltic and in Catholic Europe. Compared with his later achievements this was small indeed. At the People's Church twenty percent of the income is given to the needs and outreach of the home church . . . and eighty percent to the support of missionary effort. In 1968 the church supported three hundred and twenty-six missionaries working in countries as widely separated as Arabia and Fiji, Malaya and Mexico, Pakistan and Peru.

Oswald Smith is a hymn writer; he has written over twelve hundred of them. He is an author, three million copies of his thirty-five books have been printed in seventy languages. He is an evangelist of great power. But it is as a supporter of world-wide mission and evangelism that the world may best remember this man who once thought that if he failed as an evangelist he might have to face the prospect of being an unknown missionary in some far-off and forgotten land.

KIRCHENTAG

In 1912 terrible news reached the von Thadden family in their manor-house in Pomerania. Reinold had been challenged to a sabre duel at his university and had refused to fight!

The Kaiser's Germany was ruled by social conventions which could only be broken with disastrous consequences. One of these conventions was the duel. Amongst the students' clubs a young man's honour was likely to be judged by the duelling scars he carried on his face. To refuse to fight was to declare oneself a coward. Reinold von Thadden, son of a family whose roots in Pomerania went back to the thirteenth century, had refused on the grounds of conscience; he disagreed with duelling as unchristian. It was a reason no one took seriously. The dishonour was to haunt his life for years, both in the university and in the army.

The folly of such a judgment is shown by a life which was almost wholly dominated by physical and moral courage.

Born in 1891, Reinold followed his father's example, going to university, becoming a lawyer and a farming landowner, and taking his place as a reserve officer in the German army. By 1914, still dogged by the story of his 'cowardice', he was in the war against Britain and France, though he spent all the years in the East and in the Balkans. When it was over he returned home to Pomerania.

He could not settle down to the quietness of a rural existence. The revolutionary spirit which burned in so many ex-soldiers found a different sort of expression in von Thadden. He saw the need for the Christian gospel to take hold of disillusioned German youth, to light a new spirit of purpose in his contemporaries. He moved to Berlin to take up the secretaryship of a youth training centre, the 'Social Work Association'. Fairly quickly, with his university background—and the duel forgotten—he became linked with the Student Christian Movement, in Germany a product of the nineteenth century evangelical revival.

To von Thadden part of the importance of the SCM lay in its emphasis on the contribution of the layman to life. Christianity had to be thought through and worked out in the places where people lived.

While he was uniting one section of German youth under the Christian banner another man was busily at work fomenting a new and terrible nationalism. Adolf Hitler, almost unknown until the 1930's, was on the move. The students, and youth in general, were to become his most profitable hunting-grounds. The great *Kirchentag*—the Church Rally—of 1932 at Stettin partly organised by von Thadden was recognised by the new National Socialists, the Nazis, as the symbol of a strong Christian brotherhood which must be overthrown at all costs. The Nazis went into action against the Church.

Church elections were 'rigged'. New Nazi-sympathising clergy were 'elected' as bishops. Priests were found celebrating Holy Communion in their Nazi brown-shirt uniform, daggers by their sides. The *Horst Wessel* song rang out in place of church anthems. On the other side, Protestant and Catholic leaders, both clergy and laity, spoke against the new horror, the new disease within the nation, denouncing it from their pulpits and in their public writings. Because the official German Church was being taken over and manipulated by the Nazi heirarchy loyal Christians called out their followers from the congregations. To 'confess Christ' became an imperative reaction, and the 'Confessing Church', in effect an 'underground Christian movement', came into existence. One of its outstanding lay leaders was Reinold von Thadden.

In 1937 he was arrested by the Gestapo, set free and arrested again at the prison gates, taken to Berlin, freed and yet again arrested. The SCM was dissolved by the Nazi government. War was declared on the Confessional Church.

In 1939, Germany and Russia marched into Poland. The Second World War had begun.

Von Thadden was called up as a reserve officer. Serving first in Brittany and then in Norway, he was transferred to Belgium, where he became Regional Commissioner for the Louvain District. His humanity shone through all he did. Loathing violence, he refused to shoot hostages, gave good government to the people of his occupied district and distributed food instead of burning it when he was forced to withdraw. He was perhaps the only German officer to be publicly thanked by the Burgomaster when peace came, or to be given a public reception when he came back to Louvain.

His real troubles began when, after being invalided out of the army in 1944, he returned to his ancestral home at Trieglaff as the Russian army marched in. It was a period of tragedy and horror. Shootings went on daily in the town. Von Thadden himself was arrested, stripped, made to march thirty-five miles to the rail-head and shipped by cattle-truck to Archangel, right across the frozen wastes and steppes of Asia. Nearly half of the hundred thousand prisoners sent to the camps perished and it seemed like a miracle that he survived.

By 1945 he was back in Berlin, a half-starved skeleton knocking at the door of the courageous leader of the German Evangelical Church, Dr Otto Dibelius. From the privations and ill-treatment of those years von Thadden never fully recovered, but it did not take him long to become involved in attempting to build bridges between divided churches, hostile groups and recently-warring nations. For him the creation of the World Council of Churches was a symbol of healed wounds and future hope. But he did not pin his faith to discussions in committees. With his memory of the great church gathering at Stettin, when the Hitler Youth Movement was getting into its full stride, he began to plan for another gathering of the same kind.

He saw many values in the *Kirchentag*. It would demonstrate the spiritual power as well as the physical existence of the Church of God. It would bring people together from many parts of Germany, possibly from both East and West. Above all, it would challenge the laity of the Church to state publicly their commitment to Christian solutions of the problems which faced modern Germany. It would become a forum for the exchange of ideas and concerns. Von Thadden, who had seen both the power and the danger of massive movements in his own country, believed that the Spirit of God could use such a Christian coming-together in a most powerful way.

The first of the *Kirchentags* was held at Essen in 1950. Over 200,000 people attended. By 1956, at Leipzig, the number had grown to 650,000. Even in divided Berlin, in 1961, there were 100,000 in the West and, though the movement was forbidden in the Soviet zone under that name, churches studied the same Bible passages, listened to addresses on the same theme, faced the same questions as those in the West.

Reinold von Thadden was indeed, as his biographer called him in the title of his book, 'a man to be reckoned with'.

SERVANT OF THE POOREST
OF THE POOR

On 8th August, 1948, Mother Teresa walked out of the Loretto Convent and into the streets of Calcutta, alone. It was an unnerving experience; the beginning of something to which she had put her hand without the least idea where the Spirit of God would lead her. She had papal permission to live and work alone. For someone accustomed to the close-knit unity of convent life the freedom might have been more frightening than welcome, even though she had asked for it. She had only five rupees in her pocket. Though she had lodgings with an Indian family, that paltry sum meant that she must begin to rely on God alone to a greater extent than ever before.

She was to serve the poorest of the poor. Seen in thousands rather than in scores, the multitude of the poor presented a task which was almost overwhelming. Whom did one serve, out of all this multitude? They could not all be served. How did one choose?

She might have tried to probe the future. Would it, in five years' time, have proved worthwhile, or a failure, this desire to serve God's poorest? But that, at least, the true servant of God does not try to do. Francis of Assisi . . . John Wesley . . . Kagawa . . . Schweitzer —for them the immediate task was consuming enough. 'To serve the *present* age', in Charles Wesley's phrase, is all there is time for. The future is in the hand of God.

This slim, dark-faced nun, for the first time wearing a white *sari* instead of a habit, knew that the past had been in God's hand, too.

One of three children in an Albanian family, Agnes was born at Skopje, in Yugoslavia, in 1910. Her school was a government school, without religious instruction, but good priests kept her soul turned towards God. It was turned towards India, too, for Yugoslavian Jesuits had begun a mission to Bengal in 1925. By the time she was ten she knew that she had a vocation to the poor. The Jesuit mission meant that she saw the vocation in terms of India. She would perhaps be a missionary teacher, for she was clever enough for that. Not until she was eighteen did she respond to the suggestion that she might become a nun, instead of a volunteer. When her guidance was clearly from God, however, she has always acted decisively and in 1928 she was sent to the Loretto Abbey in Dublin for training. The following year she went to India. Her first vows were taken in 1931, her final vows in 1937.

Disciplined, devoted, to some extent enclosed within her order, she had all the security of belonging to God through His Church.

As a teacher of geography in St Mary's High School, Calcutta, she had a worthwhile occupation amongst girls who were happy, responsive and mostly well-bred. A true peasant, the contrast between these children and her village home must sometimes have startled her. The contrast between the tranquillity of the convent and its well-watered garden, bright with canna lilies, and the clamorous, crowded, struggling world outside was often in her thoughts, too. That world, rather than this, was the peasant's true world.

Not until she had been teaching for seventeen years did she become aware that God was calling her to share in it.

In 1946, travelling by train to the calm beauty of Darjeeling, with the remote grandeur of Everest and the Himalayan peaks in the distance, she knew. Perhaps she saw convent life and Darjeeling itself both as escape rather than reality. Certainly she heard God's call to the poor. Even though she asked at once, the process of release from the convent to live alone in the city was a long one. She had to write for permission to the Pope himself. At the end of two years she doffed her nun's habit and put on a white sari with a blue border and a cross on the shoulder. Sent to Patna, she had learned a little medical knowledge from the Sisters there. Already it looked like pitiable ignorance in the face of so much rampant disease in the crowded alleyways.

With her Church's permission she opened her first school in December 1948. There were five boys, and the number quickly grew. Education for those who otherwise would have had none was a natural starting point for a teacher, but clearly it would be no more than a beginning. Her first helper, a Bengali girl, joined her the following March. Something of the impact her character had made on the convent school was apparent in the years that followed. The first ten Sisters to join her mission to the poor were girls she herself had taught at St Mary's school.

Mother Teresa—already she was earning the name—was not the only person to show this concern. There were others, Catholic and Protestant, who were moved by the same compassion and, in 1950, the Missionaries of Charity were instituted by the heirarchy of her own Catholic Church. Mother Teresa has been closely linked with them, in their house in Lower Circular Road, ever since their beginning.

It is neither easy nor necessary to follow the developments of the years step by step. Nothing was planned, at any rate by Mother Teresa. Yet to her, haphazard as the growth was, everything *was* planned—by God. Her part in it was no more than responding to God in the form of the poor, the destitute and the dying.

India is not a country where much thought is given to the dying.

There are too many deaths; to care would be overwhelming. Mother Teresa herself had no specific intention of giving herself to the dying, for that matter, until she saw an old woman lying near death in the bazaar. The sight was horrible enough to turn the stomachs of even the hardened beggars—though they took no notice of the living corpse—for she was already being eaten by ants and gnawed at by hungry rats. Mother Teresa, seemingly frail but with peasant toughness, picked up the woman, smelling of filth and ordure, and carried her to the hospital. There was nothing they could do, though they dared not turn Mother Theresa away. Then, surprisingly, a medical officer of health in the municipality offered Mother Teresa the use of a *dharmsala*, a pillared hall used by pilgrims, attached to a disused temple of Kali, the destroyer-goddess. There the old woman died.

The Home for the Dying had begun.

It was typical of Mother Teresa's special sort of compassion that she should start a home for those who had no hope. No one is received into it if they have a chance of recovery. Men, women and children come there to spend their last days or hours. Beyond hope, Mother Teresa sees it as the heart of Christ's compassion that the dying of any faith or none should end their lives surrounded by love.

Always the work was for the poorest of the poor. Soon, added to the schools and the Home for the Dying, there were opened a home for abandoned children, dispensaries where the sick queued amongst the dirt of the alleyways, and in 1957 a leprosy settlement. There was no money for amenities. The leprosy sufferers made their homes in huts as squalid as most of the Calcutta outcasts. They went begging in the streets, and showed Mother Teresa their tiny gains, held out in rotted hands. But these people, unlike those in the temple, did not have to die as they would have done twenty years earlier. There is the possibility of curing leprosy as there is of curing tuberculosis. Mother Teresa had gathered skilled nurses round her. Love remained the source of her compassion but medical knowledge, educational skill and trained workers translated love into effective action.

Her Sisters accept poverty as their companion. They have only two white saris each. They have devotions at 4.30 a.m., followed by mass in the chapel where the clamour of the streets already breaks through the open windows. Then follow the chores, and a slim breakfast—how can you eat when those you serve are near to starving?—before the Sisters move off to their varied duties. Mother Teresa herself has probably had less sleep than any of them. She does her writing, endless letters to her friends all over the world, into the small hours of the morning.

In their deliberate poverty these sisters, many of them from cultured and comfortable homes, have nothing to give but themselves. They give themselves without reserve.

151

Their example is being followed in many others parts of the world. In 1965 Mother Teresa visited Venezuela to open a House at Caracas; in 1967 to Ceylon for a House in Colombo. In 1968 she opened Houses in Tanzania and Rome. In 1969 at Bourke, for the aborigines of Australia. The next year in Amman, in Jordan; and at Southall, in London, a House was opened that same year to train nurses from Europe and America. The Houses grew in number every year.

If her heart is open to the world it is also open to all who love God. There is now an Association of Co-Workers of Mother Teresa. It is open to 'men, women and children of all religions and denominations throughout the world who seek to love God in their fellowmen, through wholehearted free service to the poorest of the poor of all castes and creeds.'

The first aim of these co-workers is 'helping people to recognise God in the person of the poor'.

Another aim, exposing the vision of Mother Teresa herself, is to 'recognise the dignity, the individuality and the infinite value of every human life.'

If this sounds a solemn commitment, those who have seen Mother Teresa on one or other of her reluctant television appearances will realise that, to her and her Sisters in the Houses across the world, solemnity is hardly a word that could properly apply. Across her ascetic face sweeps laughter. Joy is in her eyes as she talks of the poor. She has her own vision of holiness, and it has something of St Francis in it.

'True holiness consists in doing God's will with a smile.'

SURGEON WITH A BROKEN BACK

Mary had always been afraid of leprosy. Christian though she was, she seemed to share the folk-belief of India that this terrible disease, which twisted men's hands and feet, deformed their faces and rendered them useless in society, was a visitation of the gods. Not, of course, that she believed in the multitudinous gods of the Hindus. Her family were members of the Syrian Christian Church, and it is the pride of that ancient church that it was founded by St Thomas the Apostle himself within half a century of Christ's death.

It was the discovery that leprosy was a disease with which she would have to deal at Vellore Christian Medical College that almost made her give up her course there soon after she had begun it. Instead, she fought down her irrational Indian horror of the disease, and worked on. That, at any rate, was typical of her character.

Once Mary Verghese had discovered the road she must travel no obstacle, however great or terrifying, would make her turn back.

Born in a landowning family in Kerala, in the old Indian state of Cochin, she proved herself a good student at her local high school and then at the Ernakulam college. By her twenty-first birthday, in 1946, she had decided to be a doctor and applied to the famous Christian college founded by Dr Ida Scudder at Vellore, a hundred miles from Madras. Twenty-sixth in a competition for twenty-five places she managed to get in because one of the successful candidates felt homesick, and left.

Affiliated to the University of Madras, Vellore had a very high reputation. Its doctors, Indian and foreign, were often leaders in their own branches of medical science. One of the most distinguished, Dr Paul Brand, was already a famous leprologist, specialising in hand-surgery, which restored skills to leprosy sufferers. In the village clinics, where Vellore staff might treat as many as five hundred patients in a one-day visit, leprosy and eye-disease figured in a large number of cases. Little by little, Mary Verghese overcame her horror of the disease and built up a reputation as a most promising student.

Some four years after she arrived at Vellore her attitude to life was transformed as she came to a point of complete Christian commitment.

By 1954 she had grown in Christian maturity. Her sense of purpose had deepened. She was a house-surgeon—an 'intern', in the American phrase—and saw surgery as her life's work. Though friends and family had married, Mary at the age of twenty-nine had turned her back on normal Indian attitudes. Instead, she was dedicated to her career.

It was on the anniversary of Mahatma Gandhi's assassination, a public holiday, that a group of house-surgeons and nurses went off for a picnic. The young driver, one of the medical staff, tried to overtake a bus on the narrow road just at a point where a stone bridge narrowed it yet further. The landrover hit the parapet of the bridge, bounced off the road and turned over into a paddy-field below.

At first they thought Mary had been killed. Instead, when they finally got her to Vellore and examined her, they discovered that her back had been broken.

Not only surgery but any sort of medical career seemed to be at an end. In India life held out no hope for the paraplegic.

Dr Paul Brand, however, had seen what such people could achieve in other countries. He described to Mary the achievements of the Stoke Mandeville hospital in England, the rehabilitation work going on in the U.S.A. and Australia, and even the Olympic Games held specially for paraplegics. An operation—laminectomy—on the lower part of her spine might well mean that Mary would at any rate be able to sit up in a chair, tied in and held upright by a special surgical jacket. Even if she could not bend there would be *some* things she could do.

But not surgery.

Yet, when the painful operation was over and the long weeks and months of exercise and physiotherapy had been endured, it was to surgery that Mary Verghese turned again. She had spent much of her convalescent period studying leprosy, and especially the way in which it affected hands and feet by seemingly destroying the muscles. As colleague of another surgeon, Dr Ernest Fritschi, Mary began to take over the hand-operations pioneered by Paul Brand. Working swiftly, her back held straight by the stiff jacket, she made incisions towards the wrist, exposed the tendons, divided them into still smaller sinews, led them under the skin to the useless, contracted fingers and thumbs, tied them in—and gave new muscular power to the useless hands. In the same way she worked with patients' feet, releasing toes once more and making walking possible.

Pain persisted. There were limitations on her ability to get about in her wheel-chair. At the same time, Mary scorned the limits her accident had imposed and would never allow anyone to engage in hero-worship. Her faith made light of impossibilities, and she was a glowing example of God's power made perfect in human weakness. There were times, however, when faith was very hard tried.

The most trying period was when she had been appointed to succeed Dr Fritschi in a research post in the leprology department and almost immediately suffered a series of complications arising from her paraplegic condition. In the end, Dr Brand performed yet one more operation to fuse and 'solidify' all the vertebrae in her spine. It gave her freedom from the constricting jacket and made operating easier, though it did not free her from pain. A new problem now arose. If she were to occupy one of the responsible posts in the department she would have to take a second degree in surgery to accord with new regulations of the University of Madras.

In her wheel chair she visited Australia, and failed in an attempt to learn to walk. It aroused new complications and she felt it was a waste of time. Then the grant of a fellowship from the World Rehabilitation Fund took her to Dr Howard Rusk's Institute of Physical Medicine and Rehabilitation in New York. It was the beginning of a new movement towards the independence her spirit craved. She learned to move from her invalid chair to bed and bath, and to waiting cars. She learned to drive a car. She specialised in those techniques which were becoming familiar in the West but remained unknown or unused in India.

Though she refused to sign a petition, soon after her accident, which could have led to the prosecution of the medical student who drove the Landrover, she never shared the sort of fatalism which saw such disasters as the will of God. They were no more within God's plan of wholeness for men than was leprosy with its tragic results of physical deformity and social ostracism. But she accepted what had happened as a test of the human spirit, an occasion for the power of God to be demonstrated. That God gave her opportunities and the courage to meet them was enough cause for thankfulness. She has never wished to be talked of as a shining example, only to be accepted as a doctor with a personal experience of human limitations and the way to overcome them.

It has been perhaps her greatest joy that she has been able to bring hope and, indeed, life itself to hundreds of leprosy sufferers as the head of the Vellore Christian Medical College's department of Physical Medicine and Rehabilitation.

THE OMI BROTHERHOOD

'Homesick, cold, lonely. But *here!*'

So wrote a young American in his diary in 1905. In the hinterland of Japan, knowing nobody, unable to speak or understand the language, he had come to teach English at a time when Japanese youth was realising that the future of their country lay in making links with Europe and America. Until that time they had been proud of their isolation and deeply suspicious of everything beyond their own traditional way of life.

Merrell Vories was to become much more than a schoolteacher. In half a century he was to be the leader of an organisation which had set up schools, a tuberculosis sanatorium, a splendid YMCA, a score of churches, a Bible correspondence course and had designed some of the outstanding buildings in modern Japan.

Born into a home with a strong missionary conscience, he resisted any pressure that he should follow a vocation of this kind. Instead he chose to take a course in architecture at Colorado College. Only when news reached America of the Boxer Rising, in which many missionaries had been killed in a revolt against western influence in China, did his mind clear. He would go to Asia—though not under any missionary society. Through the YMCA he heard of a teaching post in central Japan, at Omi-Hachiman.

Every opportunity for learning English was eagerly taken by the students and, when Vories invited boys to come to his rooms for Bible study, over forty arrived. Within a few weeks the number had risen to more than three hundred and some of those who had come merely to increase their language facility were already beginning to seek the real meaning of Christianity. The number grew steadily, proving too great for his own small quarters. He decided on a bold step. He would open a YMCA if he could get support for the project.

Help in money came from friends, and a plot of land was given by a Christian farmer with a dairy business in Kyoto.

At the end of two years Buddhist-inspired opposition led to his being dismissed from the school.

With the YMCA already organised Vories refused to be intimidated or to leave Omi. At the same time he had no means of livelihood. For a while some of his students, already at work after leaving school, came to his aid. Then, as though it were a word from God, it occurred to him in the small hours of a sleepless night that he might turn his architectural training to advantage. Why should he not begin a firm of architects here in Omi? With a single trainee, a convert from the Bible classes, he turned part of a dormitory into an architect's studio, with a table-tennis table for a drawing board. On the strength of his own skills and this small equipment the firm of 'W.M. Vories and Co.' was born.

Soon there were other trainees. Designs began to be turned into buildings. Vories quickly proved that he was an architect and technician of no mean kind. Orders started to flow in. How impressive was his success can be judged by the fact that by the time Japan entered the Second World War there were branches of the firm in Osaka, Tokyo, Seoul in Korea, Mukden, and Peking.

In 1909 he began a subsidiary company, 'Omi Sales', to import building materials, unobtainable in Japan, for sale.

Vories was on the road to public recognition and, in the normal way of affairs, to considerable wealth. He did not, however, choose to follow the normal pattern. At the beginning of the firm's existence in the YMCA he had formed a co-operative with the young men who had joined him. They shared their resources, took out their living expenses, and ploughed back their profits into a fund designed to support evangelism in the area. The province had not a single Christian congregation when Vories arrived at Omi. There were sixteen hundred square miles without a church and without effective Christian witness. The profits from the architectural firm made it possible to go out at weekends and in the evenings, holding services of witness along the forty-mile shore of Lake Biwa.

Vories belonged to no 'mission'. He disliked the idea of foreigners invading Japan, or anywhere else, to begin branches of a church dominated by overseas policies. His ideal was an indigenous church, led by its own people, expressing its theology and worship in terms of its own culture, dependent for support on its own members. In this he anticipated much of the modern thinking about 'mission'.

His firm quickly made it plain that it would provide only the best work possible, and in the shortest possible time. His office-staff would not accept bribes or 'commissions'—a lesson learned when he returned the estimate to a man who tried to promise him 100,000 yen if he got the building contract. Nor was there any work on Sundays. Again he proved the rightness of his stand when it was found that with no labour troubles, and backed by a Christian sense of responsibility, his buildings were erected more quickly than those of his competitors.

How was it possible to maintain such high, trouble-free standards?

The answer lay in the 'Omi Brotherhood'. This grew naturally out of his early trial of co-operative living and working. With a membership of over a thousand, members of the Brotherhood live together and continue their association when they are away at work. They believe that labour is a true part of community life, not a force to be exploited by masters or men. They assert that industry should concentrate on producing things which are genuinely needed by the community. The Brotherhood members accept 'a living wage', whatever their position—and the term is exact. What they do not need to live on they put back into the common fund. The earnings of each member averaged about £10 a month. Emergency needs were met from the common fund. An Executive Council, changing regularly in personnel, controls the affairs of the Brotherhood and maintains three main funds, separately registered according to government regulations. These deal with industry, architecture, and evangelism and social work.

Here, indeed, is a modern development of the New Testament practice of Christian communism. It is no longer on trial. It has been shown to work.

Part of the Vories success-story dates back to 1910, when he met A.A. Hyde in the United States. Hyde had a firm which produced a pharmaceutical product, mentholatum. So impressed was he by Vories's practicality and Christian commitment that he offered him the entire Japanese rights and, some years later, provided the funds for a Japanese factory. It was in part from these sales, as well as the architectural group, that the Brotherhood was able to engage in so much social activity—the Christian witness in practical form.

In 1917 a Buddhist monk, dying of tuberculosis, all too common in the Japan of those days, came for help. He found not only compassion but the meaning of life in Jesus Christ. Before he died he asked Vories to establish a place where other sufferers might find the same peace. As a result the tuberculosis sanatorium was begun, which was to become one of the best in Japan.

Marriage proved another step towards effective service. In 1919, summoned to provide a new home for a *daiymo*, a feudal provincial ruler, Vories fell in love with the man's daughter, who had studied for some years in America. His friends wondered what effect such a marriage would have on the Brotherhood, but they were quickly reassured. Vories and Maki Hitotsuyanagi set up home in a small hut at Omi, and almost at once Maki began to establish play-groups, kindergartens and evening classes for workers.

Bible study groups have always been basic to the Brotherhood, and they are to be found throughout the factories, in small corners as well as in the chapel at the top of one of the buildings. The aim of all study is to produce Christian leadership for a country where the traditional faiths have become, for many, no more than historic relics and hindrances to the modern way of life.

Mentholatum itself offered another means of witness. On each packet distributed from Omi was a printed notice urging the buyer to write and make enquiries about the Christian gospel. Within the first year six thousand people did so. Out of this grew the Bible Correspondence Courses. Their director was Jisaburo Yamamoto—himself a triumph of grace. An old Bible class student, he had rejected the claims of Christ to return to his father's *saki*-making firm, purveying Japan's strongest and most damaging liquor. At a riverside hotel Vories met him coming to preside over a *saki*-makers' convention and challenged him as he stepped off the boat. Embarrassed, Jisaburo first mumbled excuses and finally Poured out his unhappy story. After his conversion he joined the Omi Brotherhood and eventually took over the correspondence courses.

Vories came towards the end of his life with no money, no bank account, no worldly status. A fool for Christ's sake in the eyes of most of his contemporaries, he had given to Japan splendid buildings, sound social service, a responsible basis for living. More important, he had been able to help his Japanese Brotherhood, and many others, to preach Christ in terms that their own people could understand and respond to. In his poverty he was richer than many who scorned him and others who secretly envied his peace of mind.

It is not surprising that Toyohiko Kagawa, the outstanding Christian leader of half a century, should call him 'Japan's greatest Christian'.

'HAFFY'

During the war years Wesley Lodge, the home of the minister of New Delhi Free Church, was always crowded to the doors, especially on Sunday evenings. It was one of the few places where, like the Old House at Poperinghe which led to the formation of Toc H, rank was of no significance. In the crowd on the floor, overflowing into the study, there were likely to be staff-officers as well as privates joining in the singing, the consumption of curry-puffs, cow's hump sandwiches and cakes, and even in the washing-up. Not a few newcomers were astonished when the tall, burly man with the tea-towel put on his service jacket and disclosed the red and gold tabs of a general.

'We don't go in very much for titles here,' he would say. 'My name is Haffy. What's yours?'

Some of his colleagues on the G.H.Q. staff were not too happy about such a renegade attitude to the importance of field rank. Haffy himself found it paid in the most important way possible. It enabled him to get alongside men who needed friendship, and who perhaps needed the friendship of Christ.

None of those who were in the 'dome room' of Wesley Lodge that evening in the hot weather when Haffy gave the traditional Sunday evening talk are likely to forget it. It was not often that a speaker bared his own soul as Haffy did that night.

The beginning was ordinary enough. The story of how he came to join the army. Son of a Baptist minister, but not much impressed with religion. A scholarship to Christ's Hospital; baptism into his father's denomination to preserve him from the school's Anglicanism. 'Like some innoculations,' said Haffy, 'neither of them "took".' What 'took' much more was his love of the army. In 1916 he tried to join up and was rejected because he was only sixteen. Frustrated, he set his sights on a regular commission and was accepted for training at the Indian 'Sandhurst', Wellington in the Nilgiris. He enjoyed life more than work. Passing-in sixth in his exams he passed-out sixty-sixth. But at least he was in the Indian army, and an officer, posted to Egypt for a year. There he lived high, but managed to pay his excessive mess-bills from his bridge winnings.

India again. Poona this time, where he fell in love with Ishbal Sutherland, a nursing sister who was a deeply committed Christian. That Haffy himself was nothing of the sort was a fact he had managed to cover up successfully. After his marriage it was not so easy. Ishbal expected more than conventional churchgoing and what should have been the beginning of bliss was, in fact, the commencement of ten years of anguish. More than once the marriage was almost completely broken—and it was not his wife's fault. In the end she left him and went back to Britain with their young daughter. The pretence of even a tolerable marriage was over.

Then, in 1938, he was posted back to England—the first Indian Army officer to become a staff officer at Aldershot. They took over a flat, where he lived at one end and his wife at the other.

Such was the story Haffy told that Sunday evening. But it did not end there. In the deep silence he went on.

'That was where God took a hand. It was my job to arrange the church parades—and go to them. The chaplain, Bill Naylor, had a way of speaking to men's hearts. He spoke to mine. I knelt down in the pew one morning and prayed: "Lord Jesus, if this means anything at all, come into my heart". He did. So began for me the experience of being born again.'

For those who listened to Haffy that evening it was clear that God had taken all the qualities of enthusiasm, zest for life, administrative ability and leadership and made them His own.

In particular, prayer became the formative activity of Haffy's life.

With his Commander at Aldershot, General Alexander, he served through the 'phoney war' to the beaches of Dunkirk, where he had considerable responsibility in the massive evacuation of the British forces. General Alexander was an acknowledged Christian and Haffy made no secret of his own faith. If anyone had asked him how his division managed to feed eighty thousand troops on their way to the beaches when all supply arrangements had broken down, how they managed the final embarkation of the last seven thousand troops and cleared all the remaining casualties from the mole and from Rosendael he would have had one answer. Prayer lay behind it. After a fellow officer came across and asked if he might join in Haffy's prayers one morning this 'exercise' became as important as anything on the day's order paper. Sometimes there would be between twenty and thirty officers of the 1st Division Staff. In his own words: 'Many things went smoothly which otherwise might have gone wrong.'

The war dragged on, with its changing fortunes and new pressures as the Japanese came in on the side of the Berlin-Rome axis. For Haffy this meant long separations at a time when he would most have valued family life, but between him and his wife there was a new and unbreakable fellowship of prayer. Scotland with Combined Operations was followed by G.H.Q. New Delhi, the Dogra Machine Gun Battalion in Persia and finally Burma. The Japanese were threatening to sweep into India from Assam across the Imphal plain. 33 Corps, of which he was Quartermaster-General, was ordered to recapture Kohima, the administrative headquarters of Nagaland. In all the assaults on hills and ridges, in the plans to capture bridges before they were blown up, in the Imphal battlefield, down the Kabaw valley in pursuit of the Japanese where troops were dependent on tricky parachute supply-drops—throughout the whole campaign—Haffy met with a group of officers and other ranks for daily prayer meetings and, when they could, for Bible study. He issued a prayer-letter which noted answers as well as requests for prayer. Denominations mattered nothing. God was above all and in all.

The war over, India pressed for independence and gained it in 1947. Haffy was in Madras to lower the British flag over Fort St George. What did a discharged major-general do after a lifetime spent in arms?

He had always wanted to be a missionary from the days in Aldershot when he handed his life over to God. The opportunity came when Amy Carmichael, founder of the Dohnavur Fellowship, invited him to relieve the farmer, Norman Burns, in that centre of Christian triumph where so many children had been won from the service of the Hindu temples. Ishbal was now with him once more, but suffering from severe arthritis. Three months of the Donhavur climate was as much as she could stand. Immediately there came an invitation to take over the position of General Superintendant at the Vellore Christian Medical College. Once more it was only a year before ill-health made a return to England imperative. But during that year an immense debt was cleared and lasting friendships made with medical students who came to Bible classes in the bungalow.

Unemployment did not last for long, then or later. This time it was the Church Missionary Society which stepped in. Canon Max Warren needed a new Financial and Administrative Secretary for the Society. Haffy's reply that he had enough trouble looking after his own overdraft drew the response that he was just the man they needed: they had the biggest overdraft he had ever seen. In five years a debit of £150,000 was changed into a credit of £5,000.

It was while he was at the CMS that Sir Hugh Turnbull of the Metropolitan Police resigned as President of the London District of the Boys' Brigade. Haffy was invited to succeed him—an appointment as exciting and rewarding as anything he ever undertook. Bible classes, church services, camps and displays gave him a wonderful opportunity to get close to the boys' hearts, and he took full advantage of it, so much so that when G. Stanley Smith, son of the Brigade's founder, retired in 1951 Haffy was asked to take up full-time work as Brigade Secretary. Now the field widened to include not only the whole of the British Isles but overseas tours as well.

Retirement had proved more full of meaningful responsibility than his thirty years of Army life. In preparation for the Billy Graham London Crusades he became Chairman of the Committee, and formed a deep respect and friendship for the evangelist. A new dimension came into his own life as he saw the practicalities of personal witness and evangelism. As a result he visited the Graham team headquarters in the United States, spent time with various members of the team, shared in some of the campaigns and joined in the Australian Crusade. Treasurer of the Keswick Convention since 1959, he also became a Director of the Navigators, a less-publicised organisation, based in the USA but working amongst students, servicemen and young business executives in forty-three countries.

Nowhere did Haffy need the reassurance of prayer more than in his own home in the 1960's. His wife was seriously ill, and crippled by arthritis until she died in 1965. But four years later, after his remarriage to Miss Ruth Douglass, a former CMS missionary, a new opportunity of service began to open out. Not, this time, in world tours or in the public eye but round the Elizabethan farmhouse in which he went to live. In 1966 Ruth Douglass had started the Eddystone Housing Association to provide small homes for women who had spent their lives in the service of others. Nothing could be more to the taste of a man, still warm-hearted, friendly, cheerful and immensely able, just past seventy but seemingly ten years younger, than helping to run such an organisation.

It would probably be wrong to suggest that General Wilson-Haffenden set out to redeem the 'years that the locust had eaten', but it is certainly true that once his life was in God's hands there has never been a day when he has not been busy about the affairs of the Kingdom, nor any moment when he has doubted the power and direction of the Lord who spoke to him in Aldershot.

For further information regarding some of the organizations mentioned throughout this book, you may write to the following addresses:

Chapter 3:

> United States Foundation for International Scouting
> One Wall St., Room 2600
> New York, NY 10005

Chapter 4 (Information about the church in Burma):

> The United Methodist Church
> Board of Global Ministries
> 475 Riverside Drive
> New York, NY 10027

> American Baptist Churches in the U.S.A.
> Board of International Ministries
> Valley Forge, PA 19481

Chapter 6:

> Wycliffe Bible Translators, Inc.
> 219 W. Walnut
> Box 1960
> Santa Ana, CA 92702

Chapter 12:

> Operation Friendship, Ebenezer
> 15 Darling Street
> Kingston 14
> Jamaica

Chapter 13 (Information about Haiti):

> The United Methodist Church
> Board of Global Ministries
> 475 Riverside Drive
> New York, NY'10027

> or your own denominational mission board.

Chapter 14 (Information about Zaire):

American Baptist Churches in the U.S.A.
Board of International Ministries
Valley Forge, PA 19481

Chapter 30 (Information about the world literacy programs and Christian literature):

Intermedia
475 Riverside Drive
New York, NY 10027

BIBLIOGRAPHY

Bennett, Lerone, Jr., *What Manner of Man?* Simon & Schuster, Inc., 1968. (Martin Luther King, Jr.)

Blassingame, Wyatt, *Baden-Powell: Chief Scout of the World.* Champaign, Ill.: Garrard Publishing Company, 1966.

Daniels, Glenn, *Billy Graham.* New York: Paperback Library, 1968.

Davey, Cyril J., *Kagawa of Japan.* Nashville: Abingdon Press, 1961.

————, *Saint in the Slums.* Fort Washington, Pa.: Christian Literature Crusade, 1968. (Toyohiko Kagawa)

Davis, Elise M., *The Answer Is God.* New York: McGraw-Hill Book Company, 1955. (Dale Evans Rogers)

Hefley, James C., *Peril by Choice.* Grand Rapids, Mich.: Zondervan Publishing House, 1970. (John Beekman)

Hillcourt, William and Lady Baden-Powell, *Baden-Powell: Two Lives of a Hero.* New York: G. P. Putnam's Sons, 1964.

Huhne, Werner, *Man to Be Reckoned With: The Story of Reinhold von Thadden-Trieglaff.* Naperville, Ill.: Alec R. Allenson, Inc., 1962.

Idriess, Ion L., *Flynn of the Inland.* San Francisco: Tri-Ocean Books, 1967. (John Flynn)

Kiernan, R. H., *Baden-Powell.* New York: Argosy-Antiquarian, Ltd., 1970.

King, Coretta S., *My Life with Martin Luther King, Jr.* Holt, Rinehart and Winston, Inc., 1969.

Laubach, Frank C., *Forty Years with the Silent Billion.* Old Tappan, N.J.: Fleming H. Revell Company, 1970. (Frank C. Laubach)

————, *Inspired Letters.* Camden, N.J.: Thomas Nelson & Sons, 1956. (Frank C. Laubach)

————, *Prayer, the Mightiest Force in the World.* Old Tappan, N.J.: Fleming H. Revell Company. (Frank C. Laubach)

Luthuli, Albert, *Let My People Go.* New York: The World Publishing Company, 1969. (Albert Luthuli)

Muggeridge, Malcolm, *Something Beautiful for God.* New York: Harper & Row, Publishers, 1971. (Mother Teresa)

Nevins, Allan, *John D. Rockefeller,* ed. William Greenleaf. New York: Charles Scribner's Sons, 1959.

Northcott, Cecil, *Star over Gobi.* Fort Washington, Pa.: Christian Literature Crusade, 1960. (Evangeline and Francesca French and Mildred Cable)

Pollock, John, *Billy Graham: The Authorized Biography.* Grand Rapids, Mich.: Zondervan Publishing House, 1966.

Pope John Twenty-Third, *The Journal of a Soul,* trans. D. White. New York: McGraw-Hill Book Company, 1965.

Rogers, Dale E., *Angel Unaware.* Old Tappan, N.J.: Fleming H. Revell Company, 1971. (Dale Evans Rogers)

Sanford, Christine, *Lion of Judah Hath Prevailed.* Westport, Conn.: Greenwood Press, Inc., 1972. (Emperor Haile Selassi)

Smith, Oswald J., *Man God Uses.* Greenwood, S.C.: Attic Press, 1932. (Oswald J. Smith)

————, *Marvels of Grace.* Greenwood, S.C.: Attic Press, 1945. (Oswald J. Smith)

————, *Passion for Souls.* Greenwood, S.C.: Attic Press, 1950. (Oswald J. Smith)

————, *Story of My Life.* Greenwood, S. C.: Attic Press, 1962.

————, *Tales of the Mission Field.* Greenwood, S.C.: Attic Press, 1965. (Oswald J. Smith)

Wilson, Dorothy C., *Take My Hands: The Story of Dr. Mary Verghese.* New York: McGraw-Hill Book Company, 1963.

167